WHAT IS PSYCHOT

CW00600950

A PERSONAL AND PRACTICAL GUIDE

Second revised and updated edition

by

DEREK GALE

Published by Gale Centre Publications for

THE GALE CENTRE, WHITAKERS WAY, LOUGHTON, ESSEX, IG10 1SQ.

Tel. (081) 508 9344 - FAX (081) 508 1240

Published by Gale Centre Publications
Whitakers Way
Loughton, Essex
IG10 1SQ

© Derek Gale, 1989.

Printed in Great Britain by BPCC Wheatons Ltd, Exeter

British Library Cataloguing in Publication Data
A CIP catalogue record for this book is available from the British Library

ISBN 1 870258 01 0

CONTENTS

PREFACE

Why a personal and practical guide?

The personal and practical guides aim to help you understand what a particular therapy is about and what it feels like to experience it and to be a therapist in it. The check lists, descriptions, exercises and case histories in the guides are designed to allow you to form an individual study programme or a study programme with a group of colleagues. This programme will not turn you into therapists nor will it enable you to work on a deep level on therapeutic problems and it is not designed with either of these aims in mind. What it will do is give you an experience of how the therapeutic method works by suggesting practical exercises you can do yourself. It will also give you an experience of what it feels like to be a therapist giving that sort of therapy, the sort of problems for which the therapy can be used to help and the likely outcome.

After this study programme you will at the very least know what the therapy is about and be able to talk coherently about it. You will also have a better idea of whether you would want to be a client in that form of therapy and whether you would want to develop an expertise in it. I also hope that experienced and practising therapists will be able to find elements in the therapies described which they will be able to use to supplement and develop their own skills.

It is generally a requirement of training as a therapist that the therapist undertake therapy. It often strikes me as odd that therapists writing about their work make only scant references to their own therapy.

Therapists seem to be particularly reticent in talking about their own therapy, yet at the same time maintain that there is no stigma attached to therapy.

Therapy is not a science, it is an art and research has shown that the individual qualities of the therapist are often more significant than the method used. It seems odd that so little writing about therapy includes the personal experiences of therapists and their difficulties and failures in therapy.

The current Green revolution and the growth of interest in alternative therapies means that we are starting to pull away from the deification of scientific objectivity. This poses a problem for psychotherapy which has for so long been trying to gain acceptance by the scientific community. In its attempt to gain respectability and distance from the parodies of the actor and cartoonist, psychotherapy has used a form of scientific research and writing which alienates therapy from its true roots which are in the arts and the social sciences and not the natural sciences.

If, as I believe, psychotherapy is a search for an answer to that most fundamental of questions "Who am I", it is as much a search for a personal morality as a cure for mental pain and psychological disease. Then there is every place for subjectivity in the process itself and in books there is a place for the personal history and the personality of the author.

Humanistic psychology tends to provide more space for human error and fallibility on the part of the therapist but even in that discipline there is not enough trust for people to really be open about themselves. In this series I have made no attempt to edit out the personal approach of the authors, far less my own personality. In fact, I have encouraged them to include their personal experiences. There are plenty of books on every method of therapy written from the so called objective viewpoint and this series is offered as a counterweight to them.

The personal and practical guides do not take part in the internecine nor the intranecine battles that proliferate in most therapies but aim to put its readers in an informed position where they can make up their own mind. I welcome feedback from readers and as the books are printed on short runs can often incorporate it in future editions.

A note on Gender: to avoid the awkwardness of phrases like him/her, he/she the male authors of the series are asked to use the words he, him, etc. while the female authors use the female pronouns.

Derek Gale.

INTRODUCTION

Any book which attempts to answer the question: What is Psychotherapy? is doomed to failure, because psychotherapy is based on several different and seemingly exclusive explanations of human behaviour and several different views of how dissatisfaction with human behaviour can be resolved. To illustrate my point, let us look at the first sentence of this introduction. I have taken great care to write this in as inoffensive a way as possible, yet I am sure that there will be people who refer to themselves as psychotherapists, who will take issue with it. Perhaps they will say they are not involved in resolving dissatisfactions or that they are involved in human emotions and not behaviour.

My experience from writing the first edition of this book is that my attempt to point out the common elements of different approaches to psychotherapy, rather than the differences, did not help to form a consensus view, but did succeed in offending many of those I had sought not to offend. Where this was due to an ignorance of fact on my part, I have attempted to put this right in this second edition. However, in most cases I have realised that what people have found offensive, is the presentation without comment of the views of an opposing faction. I have taken some succour from the fact that an author who upsets all factions equally must have reached some measure of objectivity.

What I actually set out to do was to write a workbook for people in the caring professions which would enable them to explore and work towards an answer to the question: What is Psychotherapy. I wanted to do this, because there was and still is a lot of dangerous ignorance about the subject in the caring professions. The fact that I have engaged some experienced practising psychotherapists in dialogue is a bonus. As an example of the current level of ignorance, did you know that neither a psychiatrist nor a psychologist is a psychotherapist, nor are psychotherapy and psychoanalysis the same thing?

Psychotherapists themselves are often their own worst enemies in trying to resolve this ignorance, tending either to shroud themselves in mystery or advocating that their method is the only one worth considering. When, as occasionally happens, groups of psychotherapists from different factions meet, they are usually too blinkered and hostile to consider each other's points of view. Psychotherapists have a definite and marked tendency towards factionalism and internecine battles. Freud once referred to Jung as "My beloved son with whom I am well pleased", but later came to think of him as a traitor. Now the Freudian and Jungian schools have little or nothing to say to each other and are often openly hostile.

Clearly, if psychotherapists cannot explain themselves to each other, they will not be able to explain themselves to others. The effect of this has been a devaluation of the skill of the psychotherapist to the level where anybody who has, or thinks he has, a bit of psychological knowledge seems to think he is fit to be a psychotherapist. Some do not even bother to acquire the bit of psychological knowledge.

Personalities have always played a large part in the development of psychotherapy, with each new leader in the field developing a new form of therapy which he or she views as superior to all others. This is confusing to the outside observer and helps to fuel the idea that psychotherapists are cranks who do not deserve to be taken seriously.

The development in the last eighty years of a large number of types of psychotherapy has contributed greatly to the confusion about what psychotherapy is, because the methodologies of these types of therapy are so markedly different.

If a doctor and a homoeopath have a disagreement about how to treat appendicitis, it will not be difficult for an outside observer to see that they are both practising medicine, because there will be a convergence of practice. They will both agree on the cause of symptoms and that the relief of symptoms is not as important as the removal of the cause. They will both poke and prod the patient, ask questions about the pain and suggest remedial action such as pills or changes in diet and, if finally necessary, surgery. They may differ in emphasis, but they will basically be identifiable as doing the same job albeit in different ways.

However, between the psychoanalyst and the psychodramatist attempting to treat depression there is such a divergence of practice, that it will be very difficult for an outside observer to identify both practitioners as being psychotherapists and it is not much easier for the initiated observer either. The psychoanalyst in classic psychoanalysis requires a contract to meet five times a week for an hour, probably for several years and sits outside the sightline of the patient who reclines on a couch. The psychodramatist meets the protagonist (not patient) as frequently as they both decide upon, makes a strong visual and often physical contact with the protagonist, encourages the protagonist to move around and act out his problem in the here and now and meets the protagonist in a group of other people, sometimes a very large group.

Differences in methodology this large make it impossible to find a simple or even a complex definition of what psychotherapy is and it is for this reason that I have chosen to attempt an answer to the question which takes the form of a dialogue.

Some years ago I was invited to give a dramatherapy workshop for a group of psychiatric nurses in the Midlands and was told that most of them were practising psychotherapy. The first few hours of this workshop were pure hell for me because every time I suggested a simple exercise I was met by horrified stares and silent resistence. I struggled through to lunchtime and hurried off to find the person who had invited me. She listened to my tale of woe smiled and said: "But that is exactly why I invited you. They think they are practising psychotherapy in their work when they haven't got the first idea." After this I started to look more closely at what was going on in the caring professions and found that this was not an isolated pool of ignorance. People in all spheres of the caring professions considered and still consider themselves to be practising psychotherapy when they are both unqualified to do so and even haven't a clue what psychotherapy is. Some of the dialogues in this book which may horrify the knowledgeable psychotherapist are verbatim reports and others, if not verbatim, are accurate representations of the views of a very large number of people in the caring professions. Of course the situation is changing, but it is changing far too slowly and in the mean time damage is being done.

After the workshop in the Midlands I started to conceive of a workshop which would help professionals to look at their own practice, to see whether what they were doing could be described as psychotherapy and how to get training and help with improving their skills. I was extremely fortunate to have the support of Mrs. A. Cavill who was then Head of Post Basic Nurse Education at

St. Matthews Hospital in Staffordshire and who employed me to run the workshop for several of her staff. She realised just how complex a job psychotherapy is and was anxious that the nursing staff she was responsible for should be better informed so that they would not unwittingly do damage and also so that they could offer a service to their mentally ill patients, which was based in psychotherapy. As time went on, I developed course material which became the basis for this book.

It is a tremendous irony, that as I sit down to write the second edition of this book I see no further prospect of doing the workshop again at St.Matthews, as psychotherapeutically oriented training is no longer seen as a priority.

A psychotherapist is often involved in helping his clients to learn from negative experiences and transform them into positive energy for the future. In my case the discontinuation of my contract at St. Matthews has merely strengthened my conviction of the importance of this book and therefore I have substantially rewritten and enlarged it for the second edition and updated it for the revised second edition.

The structure of the book follows the structure of the workshop and is most effectively read as a workbook in which practical exercises are as important as their theoretical explanations and the reading of factual information. In a live workshop there is room for feedback and discussion after the exercises have been done and I have replaced this live discussion with notes which replace my live input from the workshops. I have attempted through this structure to draw you into trying to work out what you think, rather than laying down hard and fast rules which, as I have already pointed out, the very nature of psychotherapy makes impossible.

The book will work best for you if you skip through it first to get a general idea of the lay out and then work through it from the beginning. If possible the exercises should be done with a group of colleagues, so that there is scope for discussion.

Note to the revised second edition

When the time came to reprint this book, I reread it and wanted to change very little. Sadly the initial argument, which is that psychotherapy is an area of ignorance in the caring professions still holds true.

However, I have taken this opportunity to correct the omission of the Object Relations School and to include information about the United Kingdom Standing Committee on Psychotherapy. I have also updated the address and book lists.

I hope one day this book will become a relic, but until that time I hope it will spread some much needed light on the dimly understood topic of What is Psychotherapy.

CHAPTER TWO

THREE CHECK LISTS

The following three check lists have been written both as an introduction and as an aid to understand some of the prejudices and facts about psychotherapy. They may be used as a basis for group discussion. Each check list is followed by my own commentary on the possible answers and these commentaries are put in the place of the live discussion which followed the answering of the check lists by people in the workshops. They are similar to the answers I gave in the workshops.

CHECK LIST ONE: ATTITUDES TO PSYCHOTHERAPY

1) It is wrong to talk about feelings   YES/NO

2) It is wrong to talk about your problems   YES/NO

3) You should sort your problems out yourself   YES/NO

4) Having to ask for help is a sign of weakness   YES/NO

5) Talking to other people about your problems is dangerous
because they can end up telling you what to think   YES/NO

6) I always say what I think and mean what I say   YES/NO

7) If we have bad feelings it is because we are bad   YES/NO

8) If you have bad feelings it is right to feel guilty about them   YES/NO

9) The unconscious is just an excuse for bad behaviour   YES/NO

10) People are always responsible for what they do   YES/NO

11) It is wrong to speak or think critically about your parents   YES/NO

12) It is disloyal to speak critically of your family   YES/NO

13) The best people to help you are your family   YES/NO

14) You don't need a psychotherapist if you have a
good friend   YES/NO

15) It is a psychotherapist's job to change people   YES/NO

16) What a psychotherapist needs is common sense   YES/NO

17) What people with problems need is good advice   YES/NO

COMMENTARY ON CHECK LIST ONE

1) and 2) Psychotherapy deals primarily with the emotions: talking about them, expressing them and understanding them. It is therefore impossible to get anywhere as a psychotherapist if you feel that it is wrong to talk about emotions. In terms of therapy, the difficulties that a client feels in relation to talking about feelings and emotions would have to take up a good part of the early sessions.

(Commentary on check list one: continued)

3) Someone who comes for psychotherapy has failed to deal with his problems by himself and I doubt if anyone would come for psychotherapy because he was too lazy or self indulgent to work out his problems on his own. I have often come across the attitude in mental hospitals that a patient is only there to get attention or because he is too lazy to do anything for himself. If being in a mental hospital is a person's first choice, that is in my opinion a sign of very severe mental disturbance. Remember how in the film of *One Flew Over The Cuckoo's Nest* Jack Nicholson was disabused of the notion that mental hospitals are easy places to live.

4) It is often assumed that the need to ask for help in resolving problems is a sign of weakness. Psychotherapy responds to this in two ways. The first is to say that this sort of stiff upper lip attitude is a problem created by our society and is an attitude which is both unhelpful and undesirable. Secondly it argues that the unconscious contains material which we have repressed, because it was too painful to acknowledge. This repression has been so successful that we are, as adults, unaware that we have done it. By definition the unconscious contains material that we are unaware of and wish to remain unaware of, but have not got rid of. However, this repression of painful material, which was protective to the child, may become the adult's worst enemy because the unconscious holds on to it so hard, that it can cause neurotic symptoms. The repressed material will then have to be made conscious so that the symptoms can be rendered unnecessary. This can only be done with the aid of another person who has access to the techniques necessary to aid this process. The psychotherapist is therefore not interested in helping a person to keep his symptoms under control by stiff upper lip, but aims to find out why someone needs his symptoms, and how he can rid himself of them through understanding them.

5) Psychotherapy has safeguards which prevent this happening and it is the aim of psychotherapy to help a person work out for himself what he thinks. I have come across people who say that they have been told what to do by psychotherapists and there are examples in this book, but this is bad practice and to be deplored. Telling people what to think or to do is not psychotherapy.

6) Psychotherapy assumes that the effect of repressed material is to cause us to say one thing when actually we mean something different. Psychotherapy aims to make us aware of the underlying motivation for what we say and do.

7)8)9)10) Psychotherapy assumes that, while we are responsible for our actions, we are not responsible for our emotions. Our feelings are a response to things which happen to us and are to be understood, not criticised. It is possible that through understanding them we may be able to change our feelings or come to accept them. Guilt about our bad feelings is therefore inappropriate. Psychotherapy realises that having bad feelings does not mean being a bad person.

11)12) One of the main activities of psychotherapy is helping the client to express his negative feelings about parents and family, so this attitude, where present, would have to be changed before psychotherapy could be said to be in progress. It is sometimes suggested that psychotherapy is just a way of blaming parents for the shortcomings of the children. This is not the case. What psychotherapy does is to allow the ventilation of negative childish feelings to parents and parental figures, which were repressed in childhood.

Once these feelings have been ventilated by the adult, there are possibilities for looking at them objectively. There is such a thing as a bad parent, but even the best parents make mistakes and frustrate their children unintentionally. This has a psychological effect which psychotherapy can help to unravel.

13) Most people come for therapy because of problems with people close to them such as family and friends. While these people may be able to help the client cope and give very important support, it must be remembered that if the family is part of the problem, it is unlikely to be able to become part of the solution without outside help. As a parent who by his behaviour has contributed to a child's problem is unlikely to have done so intentionally, he is unlikely to be able to help in its resolution. In the main, families have far too much of a vested interest in maintaining the status quo to be able to help a family member change without outside help.

(Commentary on check list one: continued)

14) Friends are perhaps not as involved in maintaining the status quo as family, but they still do not possess the special skills and knowledge that a psychotherapist ought to have. Psychotherapy is not just talking to people about their problems, but a complex process of listening, questioning and interpretation. It may also involve special techniques for dealing with the material introduced in the shape of dreams, transference and overpowering feelings.

15)16)17) Very occasionally a therapist may allow himself the luxury of a piece of advice; in principle it is not a therapist's job to give advice but to help people make up their own minds. Similarly it is not the therapist's task to change people but to help them understand how they have come to be the way they are, so that they become able to change themselves if they want to.

CHECK LIST TWO: THE BASIS OF PSYCHOTHERAPY

1) If I am unaware of a feeling it doesn't exist.   YES/NO

2) The unconscious doesn't exist. I know what I am doing and do what I do because I choose to.   YES/NO

3) Dreams are just random images of the brain and have no further significance.   YES/NO

4) Dreams form a link between the conscious and the unconscious mind.   YES/NO

5) Dreams foretell the future.   YES/NO

6) We have nothing to learn about how we function from literature, fairy stories and myth.   YES/NO

7) We have nothing to learn about ourselves from studying
other cultures.   YES/NO

8) What happens to you when you are a baby doesn't matter
because babies cannot remember.   YES/NO

9) Physical pain caused to babies around the time of their
birth doesn't matter because babies cannot remember.   YES/NO

10) How babies are handled around the time of their birth

has no psychological effect on them in later life.   YES/NO

11) If the baby won't sleep it is best to leave it to cry in
its cot.   YES/NO

12) Babies and children have to have their will broken.   YES/NO

13) Memory doesn't start until about 3 years old.   YES/NO

14) How your parents responded to life's joys and
difficulties has nothing to do with how you respond to them
in adult life.   YES/NO

15) Anger is a sign of weakness or ungratefulness.   YES/NO

16) Strong emotions should be kept in check and should not
be allowed to surface.   YES/NO

(Check list two: continued)

17) It is best to try and forget painful experiences.   YES/NO

18) It is best not to talk about painful or upsetting feelings.   YES/NO

19) People who need to talk about their feelings are wet.   YES/NO

20) People cannot change.   YES/NO

COMMENTARY ON CHECK LIST TWO

1) This is perhaps the most difficult element of psychotherapy for the lay man or client to come to grips with. The psychotherapist interprets conscious behaviour as being caused by feelings which in the past the client has made an unconscious choice to repress. This explains why often people can see no rhyme or reason for their symptoms.

The job of the psychotherapist is to try and interpret how the client's feelings and behaviour in the present are indications of repressed feelings from the past. The therapist is always making hypotheses and then checking them out by putting them to the client and gauging the client's response.

2) It follows from this that the lay man may find it equally difficult to accept that actions in the present may be not only the expression of his free will, but also affected or conditioned unconsciously by his past experiences.

3) Dreams are not just random images but have specific scientifically demonstrable functions to do with physical and mental health. Deprivation of dream sleep, known as R.E.M. sleep, can cause the symptoms of mental disturbance. We all dream every night, although we may not remember most or even any of our dreams. In psychotherapy dreams are viewed as important messages from the unconscious. Freud called dreams the guardians of sleep because they prevent repressed material coming into consciousness during sleep and waking us.

4) To the psychotherapist the specific function of dreams is to form a bridge between the conscious and the unconscious mind. Interpretation of the dream symbols allows the client and therapist to understand the unconscious. Freud called dreams 'the royal road' to the unconscious. Not all forms of therapy interpret dreams in the same way, but all forms of therapy acknowledge the importance of working with dreams in one form or another.

5) Dreams may or may not foretell the future but this is not the cause of their interest to the psychotherapist.

6)7) To understand dreams and other influences on our thinking it can be very helpful to look at the meaning of the symbolism in our own literary heritage as well as how symbols are interpreted in other cultures. Jung's idea of the collective unconscious suggests that all human beings share the same 'library' of symbolic images and that these different images are to be found in all cultures.

One of the most striking differences between Jungian and Freudian approaches to therapy is to be found in the way they interpret dream symbols. Freud was interested in the freely associated train of thought set off by the dream, whereas Jung attempted to analyse the meaning for the dreamer of the symbol itself. In action therapies the dream may be acted out by the dreamer or different elements of the dream may be given an opportunity to speak through the dreamer. Some therapists may even ask the client to continue the story of the dream in the therapeutic session.

8) There used to be a very strong idea that newborn babies didn't have an emotional or sensory life and that therefore how they were treated was not of enormous significance. So, for example, up until quite recently, newborn babies had crystals put into their eyes which was obviously very painful, but, as the baby would not remember the pain, was thought not to matter.

(Commentary on check list two: continued)

9) Modern research shows that in fact babies are very aware of their environment from birth. While the adult may not remember consciously enough to relate the experience, the memory may be held in the unconscious and many psychotherapists relate problems in the present to bad births and bad handling after birth. These psychotherapists are not cranks, but unfortunately their research, much of which is reviewed in Verny's *The Secret Life of the Unborn Child*, is not widely known in Britain.

10) Melanie Klein makes great play of the relationship between the baby and the mother and suggests that the baby's attempts to make sense of this bad handling are the roots of psychological problems in later life.

11) If the baby is unhappy he will cry and if this unhappiness is not comforted or cured, the baby suffers emotionally, if not physically and does not develop a strong emotional base. This can have serious effects on behaviour in adult life.

12) Breaking the baby's or the child's will creates the sort of adults we might prefer not to have around in our society, as is argued by Alice Miller in *For Your Own Good*. Her argument is that not only does violence to the child reap its reward in violence from the child once it has grown into an adult but that the very techniques adults use to break the child's will cause the child to think that making others suffer is a good thing and "for their own good". Whatever you think of Alice Miller's theory, no psychotherapeutic system that I know of thinks that breaking the child's will is other than harmful.

13) Some people claim that memory goes back as far as the intra uterine stage of development and there is a good deal of scientific research which supports this claim. In rebirthing and primal therapy people claim to be able to recall their own birth. In any case, people not in therapy can remember events which happened well before their third birthday.

14) The need for psychotherapy is often precipitated by the failure of a person to deal with a life crisis or transition. It may well be that the client has not learnt good coping strategies from his parents. Our parents are very strong role models and we often repeat their attitudes and ways of coping or acting without even realising it.

15) Anger is a natural response. A natural response cannot be a sign of weakness. If my parents did something to make me angry, there is nothing wrong with acknowledging that fact, nor does it mean that I cannot acknowledge that they also did good things for me. To explain why we have feelings of guilt about expressing anger or criticism of our parents, the suggestion has been made that if we recognise weaknesses in our parents we may fear, that they may not be able to protect and care for us, which is too terrible an idea for the infant to bear. So to keep the parents strong we need to keep ourselves weak and assume that our parents treat us badly because we are bad and not because they are weak or feckless. To criticise our parents means recognising their failings and this we are unwilling to do. After years of lying to ourselves it can be very difficult to break the pattern. See *The Drama of Being A Child* by Alice Miller and *Depression, the way out of your prison*, by Dorothy Rowe for a further and more detailed explanation of this theory.

16) Obviously if we allowed our strong emotions to be expressed all the time, it would be very hard to get on with every day life. But psychotherapy concerns itself with the strong emotions which have been repressed and are causing problems in the here and now. As a part of dealing with these problems, powerful emotions which have been repressed, must be brought to the surface.

17)18) In terms of psychotherapy painful emotions and memories have to be recalled, faced and worked through so that their effect on present behaviour can be neutralised. Like the expression of powerful emotion, this recall may not be appropriate in every day life, but is appropriate to the therapy session.

(Commentary on check list two: continued)

19) Many people say that talking about their emotions is wet, because they are embarrassed by the process or because they haven't yet developed the strength to face the emotions and material which might come to the fore.

20) The experience of psychotherapy is that people can change, but that change is often a difficult and painful process. When a client doesn't change it is more useful to examine the relationship between the client and the therapist than to take refuge in the idea that people cannot change.

CHECK LIST THREE: WHAT A PSYCHOTHERAPIST DOES

1) In terms of training, psychotherapy is just a technique you can learn like any other.   YES/NO

2) To practise psychotherapy you don't need to have had any psychotherapy yourself.   YES/NO

3) My personal blind spots have nothing to do with how I treat clients.   YES/NO

4) I am functioning in society so I don't have to expose the painful areas in myself like the patients have to do.   YES/NO

5) Psychotherapy is properly the domain of the medical profession.   YES/NO

6) Psychiatrists are qualified to give psychotherapy.   YES/NO

7) You need a strong stomach to be a psychotherapist.   YES/NO

8) To be a psychotherapist you have to be nosey.   YES/NO

9) It is a psychotherapist's job to change people.   YES/NO

10) It is a psychotherapist's job to cure his clients.   YES/NO

11) It is best to smooth over things in the client's life
which cannot be changed.   YES/NO

12) It is not a psychotherapist's job to stir up painful
emotions in his clients.   YES/NO

13) It is a psychotherapist's job to help people adjust and
get back to leading their normal lives.   YES/NO

COMMENTARY ON CHECK LIST THREE

1) In psychotherapy learning the techniques is only the beginning. The awareness of the therapist has also to be developed. This is done through the therapist's own training therapy, through which the therapist becomes aware of the workings of his own unconscious and is therefore able to understand the client's problems without projecting onto the client. If the therapist has not had a good training therapy, he will not be aware of his own blind spots and weaknesses and will find it impossible to control and be aware of his own feelings, which will interfere with the free flow of the client's feelings. The unconsciously generated feelings of the therapist to the client are known as counter transference and in some therapies are used as an active part of the therapy.

2) It follows from this that the only way to learn psychotherapy is through being a client yourself.

(Commentary on check list three: continued)

3) Similarly it follows that my own personal blind spots do have an influence and an effect on how I treat clients.

4) This is an elegant excuse I have heard many people use in my workshops to explain why they will not talk about themselves in the way they expect their clients to. Where, in the course of the workshop, people have been able to overcome this fear, they realise that exposing problems can be liberating and not as dangerous as they thought. This gives them a greater understanding of their clients' fears and how to deal with them.

5) This leads us on to the next question, which is whether psychotherapy has anything at all to do with medicine. Many qualified psychotherapists do not have medical training and seem to be none the worse for it.

6) Psychiatrists have little or no significant training in psychotherapy in their medical training. However, they often argue that they are qualified to give psychotherapy in the way that a doctor will argue that his general training as a doctor fits him to do all medical tasks. Doctors, in my experience, will only attempt a medical procedure for which they are untrained in an emergency, but for some odd reason have no such inhibitions about psychotherapy. My parents' G.P. told me that she did her own psychotherapy for her patients by telling them to buck up and get on with life. I make no comment about this or about the fact that membership of the Royal College of Psychiatrists involves no requirement for personal psychotherapy or training therapy.

7) Some of the things a psychotherapist hears are quite horrific and if he has not learned to accept the seamy side of life and worked through his own feelings about evil, these can be very upsetting to him. If the therapist is affected to that extent by what he hears, he can not remain objective. Value judgements about what has happened to the client lead to sympathising, which is not helpful in therapy, or criticising which is even less helpful.

8) A psychotherapist has to be willing to probe what the client tells him and ask questions to encourage the client to reveal information. However, the client needs to be allowed the choice in this and not to be made to feel by the therapist that he has to tell all against his will. The therapist has therefore to be able to restrain his own curiosity and allow the client to reveal things in his own time. Voyeuristic nosiness has no place in the therapist's probing of the client.

9) On the contrary, it is not the therapist's job to change people. It is the therapist's job to help the client see how he could change himself, should he want to.

10) The term 'curing' implies that there is a physical illness which can be cured. Psychotherapy does not see mental illness as a physical disease to be cured by an active doctor and a passive patient, nor consider it possible to solve someone's problems without his active participation. In psychoanalysis there is a notion of the sick patient and a healthy therapist and Primal Therapy is called by Janov "The Cure for Neurosis", but most therapists refer to their therapees as clients, not patients, which implies that the client and the therapist are engaged in a cooperative venture.

11) Psychotherapy helps people think about painful areas in their life which they could change. It is the therapist's task to explore with the client feelings about painful areas of his life and help him to understand and come to terms with these feelings, even if the circumstances cannot be changed.

12) This is precisely the therapist's job, because through stirring up these painful emotions he can help the client to understand them. This understanding can relieve pain.

13) The client has presumably come for therapy because he feels that his life is not normal. It is therefore a moot point whether there is some normality

(Commentary on check list three: continued)

to which the client can be returned. If a woman has taken abuse from her husband for several years because she was ashamed to admit that her marriage was not perfect and then breaks down under the strain and suffers severe depression, it is hard to agree with the idea that her life was normal before her depression. In fact, it may well be her realisation that her life was not normal which will give her the strength to feel that she can change her life and therefore not need her depression. She may resist her husband's behaviour which, while her husband may not like it, strikes me as much more normal than complying with his wishes out of fear.

In my work in hospitals I have frequently heard it said that it is a spouse or parent who needs treatment, not the patient. I feel that this is a counsel of despair and that the staff in the hospital might do well to ask themselves why they feel helpless to help the client to get out of his trapped life. Often it is because the helpers can see no way out of their own traps.

CHAPTER THREE

RULES FOR A PSYCHOTHERAPIST

There are clear differences between the way a psychotherapist ought to talk to his clients and the way we talk to our friends. A therapist might say in response to you complaining about your boss: "And how does that make you feel?", whereas a friend might say: "How horrible; you better leave that job". I get very annoyed with therapists who tell people what to do instead of opening up possibilities for the client to explore his own feelings more. I have made a list of do's and dont's for discussion.

Before looking at my list it will be useful to make up your own.

EXERCISE

First close your eyes and think of a person, for example a colleague, boss or teacher, who really irritates you and think of taking a problem to him. Imagine the way he might deal with it. Think of the phrases he uses which irritate you most. Jot down the phrases.

Now repeat the exercise with someone who is emotionally close to you, such as a partner or a family member. Again jot down the phrases.

You can repeat the exercise as many times as you like.

Now look at your list. Based on the mistakes your family, friends and colleagues make, see what rules you would make up for your psychotherapist. When you have finished, you can discuss your rules with your group and make up a master list. You may decide to throw out some of your rules and include some from other people's list.

HERE IS A TYPICAL LIST:

My Headmaster at school:

1. You are not in charge here.

2. You have to do as I say even if you disagree.

3. That is not up to you to decide.

4. I know what is best for you.

5. You're upset, not angry.

My Mother:

1. Oh dear!

2. Well, I don't really understand that.

3. I am tired.

4. We'll see what your father has to say.

My Father:

1. Don't let on to your mother.

2. (An image of him laughing at me when I am upset)

3. I'll sort that out for you.

Rules from this list:

1. There are a lot of people telling me I am not in charge of myself, so I want a therapist to treat what I feel and say seriously, however stupid I may feel it to be. My rule would be: **Listen to the client, don't talk as if you know best.**

2. The feeling that other people knew what I felt better than I did myself, is very strong, so my second rule would be: **Value the client's perceptions of how he feels.**

3. There seems to be a lot of pushing responsibility on to others, so my third rule would be: **Take responsibility for your part in the relationship with the client.**

This exercise can be very useful as a piece of self exploration as well as a training exercise.

RULES FOR A PSYCHOTHERAPIST

If you can honestly say, that in your professional practice you keep all the following rules, then you are a very skilled psychotherapist. I have developed this list of rules, because people in the workshop often tell me they thought they were giving therapy, but now realise that they were giving advice or worse, telling their clients what to do.

These rules can very usefully be used as the basis for a piece of self supervision or peer group supervision. By tape recording a session WITH THE CLIENT'S PRIOR CONSENT, you should listen to five minutes of active dialogue, ticking off any examples of rules you have broken. Go back over the dialogue and try and work out for yourself why you said what you said and how you could have reacted differently.

DO

1. Listen to the client. This may seem obvious, but it is amazing how often we don't really listen to what the client has said before we jump to conclusions about it. Whatever the cause of our impatience, whether it is a wish to help or boredom, we have to learn to keep it under control. It is very important for the client to feel that he has been really listened to and properly understood, so the therapist must take as much time as he needs to listen to the client.

2. Ask questions if necessary, to make sure that you have really understood the client properly. Don't be inhibited by thinking the client will be offended. The psychotherapist needs to be sure of the situation, more than he needs to seem polite or infallible.

3. Encourage the client to open up by asking questions, rather than by telling him to do so. The more the client is able to reveal his own feelings, the deeper and the more healing will be the level of work.

4. Offer alternative explanations to the one favoured by the client for him to consider. It is the therapist's job to challenge the client's perceptions, but not to force his views onto the client.

5. Keep questioning yourself about your own motives. If you are acting as a therapist to fulfil your own needs rather than those of your clients, you won't get far. The truth is, that however good we are as therapists, our own unconscious is always trying to intrude, which is why our own therapy and a training therapy are so important. They help us to be aware of our own unconscious and to keep it under control in the therapeutic relationship.

6. Be aware of the wider context in which therapy is taking place. Everybody who comes for therapy has a life outside of therapy. The practicalities and pressures of that life can be very different from the practicalities and pressures of the therapist's life. A client of limited means with children, for example, may find it much more difficult to get to therapy on time than a therapist who has an au pair and a car.

7. Be open to the possibility that there may be an alternative and possibly better explanation to the one that you favour. The therapist is not always right and sometimes the client is right. Also there is not much point in forcing an interpretation on a client, who just isn't willing or able to hear it. A client will not gain confidence in you for forcing your views on him, no matter how right they are.

8. Reflect back to the client what he has said. This is much more effective than criticising the client.

9. Always allow and encourage the expression of the client's feelings, even if they are very strong and uncomfortable for you to hear. Clients often bring up material which is uncomfortable for the therapist to experience. The therapist has to be careful not to inhibit the client by unconsciously giving the client signals that the therapist can't cope.

DON'T

1. Don't give advice. Apart from the fact, that if it turns out to be bad advice, the client will blame you, the function of therapy is to make the client independent and capable of making up his own mind, not dependent on you for advice. It is the therapist's job to help the client see all the sides of a problem and to show the client how he is capable of deciding for himself, either by following his feelings or weighing the advantages and disadvantages on the available evidence. Also and perhaps more important than all the rest, the function of therapy is to help the client realise what are the underlying causes for his inability to make up his own mind.

2. Don't tell people what they are feeling. It is the psychotherapist's job to listen to what the client is feeling. There may be times when you say something like: "I think you may be feeling...." but this is an invitation, not a direct statement. Paradoxically, the more space you leave for the client to say what he wants to, the more the client will feel able to reveal and the deeper the level of work will be.

3. Don't talk about your own experience. Telling the client that you have had just the same feeling or experience, takes time away from the client and usually makes the client feel that he has to become a therapist to the therapist. All of this makes it more difficult for the client to explore his own feelings. On the other hand, knowing that the therapist knows how the client feels can be very helpful.

4. Don't devalue symptoms. In an attempt to reassure the client, the therapist might say "Oh, lots of people feel like that" or: "That's not serious; I've felt that way myself." It can often be helpful for the client to know that he is not the only person in the world with that particular problem, but if a client raises a symptom or a problem, he is indicating that for him it is very important, however trivial or normal it may seem to the therapist.

5. Don't give or make value judgements. There is nothing more inhibiting to a client than the feeling that the therapist is judging him. If this feeling is based in reality, therapy will come to a rapid halt. The whole idea of therapy is, that it is a place and a time in which I can air my innermost guilts without being punished for them.

6. Don't take criticism personally. It is important to understand that criticism of the therapist by the client is a communication from the client, which can be reflected back to the client to help him understand his problems. If the therapist takes criticism personally, he misses what the client is trying to say. An example is necessary here to make the point clearer.

1.) Client: *I hate those ties you wear. They show what poor taste you have in fashion. I can't trust you.*

Therapist: *What I wear is none of your business. Please keep your views to yourself.*

    SILENCE

Alternatively:

2.) Client: *I hate those ties you wear. They show what poor taste you have in fashion. I can't trust you.*

Therapist: *I see. Does my taste in ties remind you of anyone you know?*

Client: *Yes, my father used to wear the most horrible ties.*

    QED

    I am not one of those people who say that all critisism of the therapist by the client is transference. Sometimes the therapist is wrong and then it is best if he admits it. But if the therapist identifies with the client's criticism, the value of the criticism for the client's therapy is lost.

(Rules for a psychotherapist: continued)

7. Don't assume that you are in some way superior to the client. The medical model of a sick patient and a healthy client is particularly prone to this interpretation of the client as somehow weak and inferior to the strong and superior doctor therapist. Both the therapist and the client are engaged in a cooperative struggle to understand how and why the client's problems have occurred and in this investigation the client is as important as the therapist.

8. Don't blame the client. The therapist's job is to help the client understand his feelings and actions. Blaming doesn't aid understanding, it merely increases guilt. Part of the job of therapy is to help the client loose inappropriate or crippling feelings of guilt.

8. Don't confuse mental illness with stupidity. A story which I first saw in Bruno Bettelheim's *A Home for the Heart* illustrates this point beautifully:

A car develops a puncture outside an insane asylum and the driver gets out to change his wheel while being observed through the wire netting by the inmates of the asylum. Just as he is about to put the nuts back on the wheel, he sees them roll down a nearby drain.

"Damnation!" he says out loud, "how in hell am I going to get home if I can't bolt the wheel back on." He stands there for a few moments scratching his head until one of the inmates calls him over and says:"If you take one nut from each of the three remaining wheels, you will be able to bolt the wheel on and drive slowly to a garage for help"."Of course", replies the driver. "How stupid of me. It's me who should be inside, not you."

The inmate replies: "That is just where you are wrong. We are in here, because we are insane, not because we are stupid."

For more examples of how the rules are broken and often by people who should know better, turn to the dialogues in the next section.

CHAPTER FOUR

DIALOGUES

In the workshop I play participants recordings of simulated therapeutic sessions and ask them to spot the mistakes. The dialogues are made up and exaggerated to make a point, but in fact they are based in real life and when I play them in the workshop, participants are generally able to identify people they know, who frequently make these mistakes. As I run the group mainly for psychiatric nurses, the examples relate to psychiatrists. However, all of the caring professions have members who make similar mistakes because they believe that psychotherapy does not require special training.

The dialogues should be read in conjunction with the chapter 'Rules for a Psychotherapist'. As a teaching aid it can be useful to note which mistakes are made in each dialogue as a preliminary to discussion. The mistakes are listed at the end of the chapter.

Dialogue 1

Doctor: *Good afternoon Mrs Jones. I understand you're suffering from depression.*

Patient: *Yes.*

Doctor: *Do you feel depressed all the time?*

Patient: *Yes.*

Doctor: *I see. So you don't have any times when you don't feel depressed?*

Patient: *Not really.*

Doctor: *Well... Why don't you go out and enjoy yourself now and again?*

(Dialogue 1: continued)

Patient: *It doesn't seem to work like that, doctor. I don't even seem to be able to get myself together to go out.*

Doctor: *I see. Well, why don't you sometimes get up in the morning and let me see, ah yes, get some make up on, pretty yourself up and then you could go out and do some shopping and buy yourself a new dress.*

Patient: *But I don't like shopping and I feel as though I can't face my friends. Shopping really does make me feel depressed. And if you don't mind me saying, I...um...do get up, and get made up in the morning and dress properly if I feel up to it.*

Doctor: *Well, if you don't like shopping, why don't you....*

The conversation develops and the woman talks of her voluntary work commitments and the interview ends with the therapist saying:

Doctor: *You had better give up the voluntary work. It is obviously too much.*

Patient: *Yes, but I don't want to, it's just that I feel so depressed.*

Doctor: *You give it up and rest.*

Patient: *Yes, but...*

Doctor: *You do as I say and you'll feel better. Come back and see me in three months.*

Patient: *Thank you so much for telling me what to do doctor.*

Dialogue 2

Doctor: *Hello Mrs. Smith.*

Patient: *Doctor, I have a very responsible job and recently I have been panicking and losing sleep and now I don't seem to be able to do my job properly.*

Doctor: *Well, of course a lot of people worry about their work, you know.*

Patient: *Yes, but this is quite excessive. I lie awake at night and worry about the simplest phone call I have to make to a client and when it comes to talking to people on the phone my hand is shaking so much I can hardly dial the number and hold the receiver.*

Doctor: *Well, a lot of people don't like using the phone, you know.*

Patient: *But I haven't always been like this. It's a recent problem and I am getting worried about it because it's affecting my work.*

Doctor: *Are things going well with your job otherwise ?*

Patient: *Yes, they are.*

Doctor: *Well, I must tell you, a lot of people with important jobs do get nervous.*

Patient: *Yes, but it's a totally irrational fear. I even worry that my clients are going to sexually attack me.*

Doctor: *Well, I am sure that there are a lot of women who worry about that these days. We live in a violent society.*

Patient: *Yes, but I am capable of looking after myself and...*

Doctor: *Well, there you are. There is nothing to worry about. You stop worrying and if you can't sleep in a week or two I'll tell your G.P. to give you some sleeping pills.*

Dialogue 3

Doctor: *Well, Mrs. Shah, you want to talk to me about your problems.*

Patient: *Yes. My father died while I was away on holiday.*

Doctor: *Where were you away on holiday?*

Patient: *I was on a walking tour in Yorkshire.*

Doctor: *Well, that's a strange coincidence. You know, my father died while I was on holiday. I was with friends too, but abroad.*

Patient: *They couldn't reach me because we didn't have a fixed route and by the time I was contacted it was too late.*

Doctor: *They got me in time, but I was on a package tour and I couldn't get a flight back before he died. It was very upsetting.*

Patient: *Yes.*

Doctor: *I still have symptoms from it now.*

Patient: *Yes.*

Doctor: *It is very upsetting.*

Patient: *Yes I know and...*

Doctor: *I still imagine he isn't dead, which is strange, because I went to the funeral.*

Patient: *Yes, if I could just tell you...*

Doctor: *I saw him being buried.*

Patient: *Yes, I see. Was he an old man ?*

Doctor: *Not very old really.*

Patient: *And your mother?*

(And so on till the patient gets her prescription)

Dialogue 4

Doctor: *Hello Mrs. Brown. Now that you've been in the hospital for a couple of weeks, I thought it would be a good idea for us to have a chat.*

Patient: *Yes.*

Doctor: *Now how are you getting on? Plenty of visits from your husband?*

Patient: *No, actually, he hasn't been at all.*

Doctor: *Oh how awful. Why ever is that?*

Patient: *Well, we haven't seen each other for ten months.*

Doctor: *Because?*

Patient: *Well, we weren't getting on together and so we separated.*

Doctor: *That's good and did that improve matters? Are you having trouble getting the children looked after while you are in hospital?*

Patient: *Oh no, they live permanently with my husband.*

Doctor: *Housing problems?*

Patient: *Well, we thought it better...*

Doctor: *Better for the children not to live with their mother? Children should always be with their mothers.*

(and so on)

Dialogue 5

We enter in the middle of a regular therapy session for an in-patient.

Patient: *There is something important I wanted to tell you and I have wanted to tell you for some time.*

Doctor: *Good. That is what I am here for.*

Patient: *Yes, but you might not like it.*

Doctor: *Of course I will. You need to tell me all the things you feel you can't tell anyone else and that will cure you. That's what I am here for.*

Patient: *Well, I want to tell you that I am annoyed.*

Doctor: *Yes...*

Patient: *Angry, actually, very angry, very angry indeed.*

Doctor: *Splendid. Now we are getting somewhere. Who with?*

Patient: *With you.*

Doctor: *With me?*

Patient: *Yes. I am very angry with you, because you never give me a chance to say what I want to say and I decided that today when we met I would tell you how angry I felt after the last session.*

Doctor: *Well, you've told me now dear, so let's get back to talking about you.*

Patient: *No! This IS about me.* (raising her voice) *I want to tell you about how angry I felt, because you never give me a chance to say what I want and you just tell me what to do.*

Doctor: *Now just calm down...*

Patient: *No I won't. I want to tell you how ANGRY I feel.*

Doctor: *You're obviously getting very upset and upsetting yourself unnecessarily.*

Patient: *It's not unnecessary.*

Doctor: *Now just listen to me. Perhaps I need to increase your drugs.*

Patient: *No. I am always listening to you. I don't need drugs. You're just like my father. He used to say that all the time.*

Doctor: *I think you better go back to the ward before you get more upset.*

NURSE! NURSE!

Patient: *I don't want to go back to the ward. I want you to listen to me.*

Doctor: *Ah Nurse, take this lady back to the ward and I'll be up in a minute to write her up for something to calm her down.*

Patient: *No, I want you to listen to me.*

Nurse: *Just come with me and everything will be OK.*

COMMENTS

Dialogue 1

1) The 'Why don't you then you'll feel better' syndrome

2) Sexist assumptions: prettying herself up and shopping will cure her

3) Telling the patient what to do

4) Taking away her only prop, the voluntary work

Dialogue 2

1) Devaluing symptoms

2) Drawing interview to a close when it doesn't go the psychiatrist's way

3) Recourse to the G.P. and medication

Dialogue 3

1) Talking about his own problems

2) Not allowing the patient to speak

Dialogue 4

1) Time elapsed too long before interview

2) Patient's view not canvassed

3) Patronising tone

4) Critical value judgments

Dialogue 5

1) Cure?

2) Inability to handle patient's anger

3) Recourse to drugs

4) Missed transference: ' You are just like my father'

5) Passing problem to the Nurse

CHAPTER FIVE

CHARLATANS WELL INTENTIONED AND OTHERWISE

Psychotherapy often seems to be viewed as something anyone can do and hardly a worthwhile profession for somebody who could manage a more important job. At the present moment there are no nationally accepted criteria for qualification as a psychotherapist. Anybody can quite legally call himself a psychotherapist without there being any necessity for him to have a qualification and without there being any supervision of his work.

The United Kingdom Standing Conference for Psychotherapy has developed out of the Rugby Conference. It represents 65 training organisations and intends to frame regulations which will be guidelines for future legislation in the U.K. and negotiations with the E.E.C.

I do not intend to dwell on the proliferation of cranks and charlatans, some of whom are out to make a quick buck. Fortunately the public do not seem to be as gullible as it is sometimes assumed to be and these people do not stay in business long, unless they have some genuine service to offer. I find more seriously worrying the practices of people who have a recognised qualification in one of the caring professions and a job which puts them in a position of trust. These professional qualifications are not a qualification in psychotherapy and a doctor, social worker or educator who claims to practise psychotherapy while remaining blissfully ignorant of what psychotherapy really is, trades on the public's confidence in his profession and is therefore as great a charlatan as the person who holds a bogus diploma.

The following conversation is based on a real conversation which took place between myself and a psychiatric registrar working in a mental hospital. The training program referred to in the conversation was a course put on by a major teaching hospital to qualify him as a member of the Royal College of Psychiatrists. I have since checked this story with him and found the subsequent conversation even less reassuring as he told me that he doesn't consider the course to have qualified him in analytic psychotherapy, only in dynamic psy-

chotherapy, a statement which is totally meaningless. The way he freely ban-
died these terms about was nearly as frightening as his astonished tones which
implied that no sane person would want to have anything to do with psychotherapy anyway. Fortunately he also pointed out that his practice today does not involve psychotherapy as he is involved in more medical aspects of psychiatry with
people who have a mental disease such as brain lesion.

One day he mentioned in passing that he had a patient coming for psychotherapy and when I asked him about this, questioning whether he was qualified to give psychotherapy, he replied:

Doctor: Yes. I am a doctor and also it is part of our registrar training programme.

Me: Really, I am fascinated. Tell me more.

Doctor: Well, there are a number of us and we meet once a fortnight with a
qualified therapist for an hour and a half and each of us present our case in
turn.

Me: So how often do you present your case?

Doctor: About every twelve weeks and it's my turn next week.

Me: And how much individual therapy have you had prior to starting work
with this woman?

Doctor: None. I don't need therapy. I am not sick.

Me: And group therapy?

Doctor: Look Derek, it's my patient who needs therapy, not me.

Me: So you have had no experience as a client?

Doctor: That's right and I don't need it just to give psychotherapy.

Me: And have you had any other training in psychotherapy?

Doctor: I don't need training for this woman to tell me about her problems,
it's up to her to talk to me. I've read a couple of books off the reading list.

Me: Do you then interpret what she says?

Doctor: I don't go in for that sort of thing, I rather advise her on what she
should do about her problems. It's good for her to talk about the things that
worry her.

Me: How do you handle transference?

Doctor: Transference? Oh I don't go in for all that technical stuff. We just talk about her problems.

Me: But that isn't psychotherapy. She could do that with her next door neighbour.

Doctor: Look, I haven't got time to stay here gossiping all day. I have got patients to see. Anyway I don't think psychotherapy is doing my patient much good anyway.

Me: (silently) That might be because she doesn't seem to be receiving any.

I have quoted this conversation at length to show how the process of therapy is often viewed by the medical establishment.

The activity being undertaken by this registrar can by no stretch of the imagination be described as psychotherapy nor can the seminars he attends be described as more than an introductory and cursory piece of training.

There is no sense in which the doctor is having his own experience of therapy either as a client or trainee. Nor is there an appreciation of what material in the session is significant and how to handle it. The conversation shows the low esteem in which a large part of the medical profession holds psychotherapy.

If you are interested in trying to understand the prevalence of this attitude to psychotherapy in the medical profession, you should read the book *Basic Psychotherapy* by Parry, which is a text highly thought of by doctors. It is written by a doctor, whose superior attitude and lack of understanding of what psychotherapy is, make this just the sort of book which encourages and perpetuates this attitude and practice.

CHAPTER SIX

HOW TO CHOOSE A PSYCHOTHERAPIST

The further you read through this book, the more clear it must become that choosing a psychotherapist and finding one who knows what he is doing, is not going to be an easy job. If you have had therapy before, you may not know why it has broken down and these questions may help you to make up your mind. If you intend to train as a therapist you will find these questions helpful in making a choice of training. If you have never had therapy before, try and use them to form a dialogue with the therapist and be guided by him to make up your own mind. In this section I will outline a number of questions you can ask your therapist and yourself.

EXERCISE

Before going on to read this section it might be a good idea to try and write down the questions you would like to ask your prospective therapist and also what criteria you would find important in choosing a therapist. If you are working in a group you can discuss these in the group before looking at my ideas.

It is unlikely that your therapist will be able to fulfil all the criteria I list and therefore you will have to make these questions the basis for a dialogue with a prospective therapist. It might seem unusual to cross question a professional about his competence before engaging him, but apart from the problems caused by the lack of registration of therapists, the therapeutic relationship is such a personal one that it is as important for the client to interview the therapist, as it is for the therapist to interview the client.

QUESTIONS TO ASK THE THERAPIST

1) Is the therapist willing to talk to me about his qualifications, methodology and training?

I would view with some suspicion a therapist who refused to answer questions about his professional competence at an initial interview. It is often hard for the therapist to take questioning from the client, but if he cannot deal with it now, how will he deal with it when the transference gets going? It can often be possible for the therapist to include and use these questions to make the client's doubts and resistances clearer.

2) Is the therapist trained in psychotherapy?

It might seem a bit rude to ask the therapist about his training, especially if you are having therapy in the N.H.S., but as we have already seen, we can not assume that because someone offers psychotherapy he is trained to give it. Indeed, it is within the N.H.S. that the least qualified people most often think of themselves as being able to offer therapy.

There are many different training courses in psychotherapy and many very skilled therapists started work before there were formal training programmes easily available, so it may be necessary to probe with your prospective therapist what training he has had if he does not have a formal training qualification. If his answer is: "I don't have a paper qualification, but I have read a lot and picked it up as I went along", proceed with caution. If, however, he has had a long period (over 3 years) in therapy and supervised practice afterwards, he is probably quite competent despite a lack of paper qualifications.

3) Is the formal training recognised and if so by whom?

There are very few recognised university degrees in psychotherapy and most qualifications are not validated by an external validating body such as the C.N.A.A. However, this does not mean that the qualification is worthless. Membership of a professional body is an indication of competence, although not all professional organisations are as professional as they should be. A number of professional bodies and training courses are listed in the section on training.

These are ones which I consider to be safe, although the list is not totally exhaustive and when you come to read this book, it might be out of date. A good indicator might be to check whether the organisation is a member of the United Kingdom Standing Conference for Psychotherapy.

The answers given by your therapist to the rest of the questions in this section will help you to make up your mind regardless of paper qualifications.

4) Has the therapist had his own personal therapy?

I would go so far as to say that no therapist is worth consulting, unless he has had a good long dose of personal therapy. The question of course is: How long is long enough? As a fixed point one might usefully take three years as a jumping off point. I favour an extended period with one therapist and this is becoming more and more the norm; however, some forms of therapy, such as psychodrama and Gestalt therapy, do not insist on this.

The fact that a therapist is still having personal therapy is not a sign that he is no good. It is often a plus point, because it means he is still open to examining and developing himself. In fact, in my own professional organisation continuing personal therapy is a condition of membership.

5) Supervision

If a therapist does not have supervision, the chances are that he is not remaining objective. Some very experienced therapists seem to get away without supervision and be none the worse for it, although even they probably consult someone from time to time. A newly qualified therapist should have supervision weekly and one who has been practising for a few years should have regular individual supervision, peer supervision or peer group supervision. Don't be afraid to ask.

6) Gender

Deciding on whether you want a male or female psychotherapist can often be a complex problem for two reasons. Firstly, the client may have a genuine need for a therapist of one sex, but also making a choice can be a sign of the client's resistance. Secondly, once therapy is under way, the sex of the therapist may be irrelevant.

The sex of the therapist may be important to you and the therapist may ask you about this himself. If you are seeing a man and want to be seeing a woman, it is worth asking whether there is a female therapist available. Some therapists don't consider this important, but if it is important to you, it should be taken seriously by the therapist. If it isn't, perhaps other issues you take seriously aren't being given their full value by the therapist.

7) Money

Psychotherapy in the National Health Service is usually free, but in settings where you have to pay, it is a very rare therapy relationship which does not have problems over money. Therapy is an expensive business in which missed sessions are usually charged for. Make sure that you get the financial arrangements clear before you start.

I don't advise people to take on therapy they cannot afford. That is merely increasing the number of problems they have. I do often take clients who cannot afford my full fees and most therapists have a way of accommodating clients who cannot afford full fees. Don't be afraid to ask.

I have not generally found it successful to take services of a different kind from clients in lieu of payment e.g. baby sitting or gardening. I am quite sharp with people who tell me they cannot afford therapy while supporting an otherwise extravagant life style.

I generally find that problems about money in therapy are a reflection of other problems in the therapeutic relationship. In the N.H.S. clients often transfer their feelings about money to time, i.e.: "This therapy is wasting my time", rather than "This is a waste of money". Therapy is about discontent and in therapy discontent is divine.

8) Times

Some therapists are willing to negotiate times, others insist on a fixed time every week. Before committing yourself to either type of arrangement, make sure it suits you. Committing yourself to paying for a fixed time each week can be very reassuring, but also infuriating if your job or other commitments mean that you miss sessions you have to pay for. If you can cope, the infuriation you feel may be very therapeutic; however, if you know that you won't be able to stick to a fixed routine, you are committing yourself to an arrangement which is bound to fail from the start.

9) Session Length

Therapists differ over this. Most people offer a therapeutic hour lasting fifty minutes. Less than this seems to be a bit of a con, unless charges are adjusted accordingly. Some therapists offer or use a method which requires longer sessions, sometimes as long as two or three hours. If you have strong feelings about this, discuss it at the initial session.

10) Accepting a trainee

You can often get very good therapy from trainees, because they have fewer clients and are very closely supervised, as well as being cheaper.

After having done this exercise, you can increase your understanding of the problem both from the therapist's and the client's point of view by doing the role play below.

ROLE PLAY

Split the group into threes. One person plays the role of the prospective therapist, the second plays the role of the prospective client and the third takes the role of observer. If there is no observer, a tape recorder can be a good idea.

The instructions for this role play are that the prospective client and prospective therapist talk about how therapy might go. Developments can include thinking of why he is going for therapy and even thinking out a role and history for the client. The therapist can also decide on a character, either obstructive or helpful for example.

The role play can work very well if the role players model themselves on specific people they know. It can be even better if they can role play specific problems that they have had.

KEEPING YOUR THERAPIST or HOW THE CLIENT OUGHT TO HANDLE TRANSFERENCE

EXERCISE

Before reading this section it will be helpful to make a list of the feelings you have when you doubt your therapist's competence or genuineness and the things you do. Discuss it before reading my comments. A typical list follows.

WHAT I DO WHEN I DOUBT MY THERAPIST'S COMPETENCE

1. Panic.

2. Feel I can't discuss it with him.

3. I must change therapists.

4. But I've got to discuss it with him first.

5. He'll throw me out if I tell him what I really feel.

6. He'll only say it's transference and I know its really him I'm angry with.

7. He's no good as a therapist.

8. I'm no good as a client. It's all my fault.

9. I've got to protect him from my bad feelings.

10. Arrive late. Cancel the session at the last minute.

In the early stages of therapy there is usually a honeymoon period in which the client makes progress and feels confident about the therapist. However, after a period of time the client may start to feel stuck and to doubt the therapist and even to feel that the therapist is doing positive harm. This, with a good therapist, will be what is known as transference and with a bad therapist a sign that the client should get the hell out and quick. Unfortunately for the client it is very difficult to distinguish the one from the other and while successfully working through transference is very healing, staying with a bad therapist is downright dangerous. The problem about this for the client is that there is really no one to discuss the problem with.

A typical scenario might go something like this:

"My mother was shocked when I told her I was having therapy and made me promise not to tell my father and my wife used to be in favour of my having therapy, but now keeps going on about the cost and saying that she doesn't think it's helping. I've mentioned that I am having therapy to my friends and they think I am crazy to waste my money on it. Into the bargain I dare not tell my therapist how I feel, because he will throw me out."

To the dispassionate observer the client's dissatisfactions might be clearly identifiable as transference, but on the other hand there is always the possibility that the client is right and that the therapist is no good or no good for him.

The client feels despairing and trapped and there seems no way out of the trap. If he leaves the therapist, he will never know who was right and the therapist will have got off the hook far too easily and if he stays, the therapist may continue to do him real damage.

For the client the problem is magnified by the fact that he can't get his thinking clearly sorted out and make a clear decision. It is all surrounded by if's and but's.

Fortunately I have a golden rule.

Whatever the problem is in therapy, first discuss the matter with your therapist. No matter how aggressive, rude or horrible what you want to say to your therapist may feel to you, if you feel it, you should be able to share it with your therapist.

If your therapist refuses to discuss your feelings with you, then you are best off finding another therapist, BUT be careful: your therapist may well try and feed your feelings back to you and in so doing is attempting to help you understand them and own them as your own.

If your therapist rejects you for disclosing what you feel, then you have lost nothing and had better find another therapist quick, because all forms of psychotherapy require the therapist to be able to hold safely the client's most uncomfortable feelings.

It may be that the therapist will acknowledge that your doubts are well founded and that he has been at fault. Sometimes it is possible for this situation to be recouped and sometimes it is necessary for the client and therapist to agree that a change to a different therapist would be a good idea.

Clients do outgrow therapists and often a change of orientation to a different therapist or even a different type of therapy can be helpful. At certain points it can also be useful to change to a therapist of the other sex.

On the other hand, in my opinion it can be very helpful if the client and therapist can go on talking about the client's dissatisfactions until they are resolved in some way which the client finds satisfactory. It may be very important for the client to be able to criticise the therapist at great length in a way which he was never allowed to criticise his parents.

What if I change therapists?

There can only be one reason for not changing therapists and this is that my dissatisfactions are my problem and not the therapist's lack of expertise. If the problem is mine, obviously the same problem will recur with any other therapist I choose to work with. Many therapists take this as a counsel of despair, but I differ from them over this because if I have to reject ten therapists before I recognise that the problem is mine, not theirs, then that is what I have to do and there is nothing I can do about it. In my view none of the experience with the first ten therapists will be wasted.

It may be possible for the client to test out whether his feelings about the therapist are objective or transferred, by asking himself whether in some way the therapist is behaving "just like my mother" or "just like my father" or both. The power of the transference as a healing force is not lost by realising that it is transference. The important thing is how strongly the feelings are felt by the client and the transmitting of these feelings to the therapist, so that however painful it may be, they are out in the open and can be discussed.

I advise caution of a therapist who cannot let go of his clients. Some therapists become extremely possessive about clients and find it hard to let go or even countenance letting go of a client. I often find that if I can honestly tell a client that it is up to him whether he leaves or stay and that I will respect his decision and support him in it, this gives him a freedom which helps him to view the problem much more clearly.

Apart from being possessive, there may also be economic reasons why a therapist might not want a client to leave and I agree with Mario Jacoby who says in *The Analytic Encounter* that for this reason it is a good idea for a newly qualified therapist to have another source of income while building up his practice. As Jacoby points out, if the therapist is dependent on the client he may well avoid certain material for fear of offending and therefore losing the client. This is good neither for client nor therapist.

ROLE PLAY EXERCISE

This role play can be spoken into a tape recorder or take the form of a letter if you have no partner. You, the client in therapy, are telling a friend or colleague about all the things that are going wrong in therapy and which you are unhappy about. This role play can work really well if you are willing to let yourself rip and be really outrageous.

Afterwards you can discuss with your partner what your complaints mean and whether they are justified or part of what your problem really is.

PSYCHOTHERAPY IN PRACTICE

This is an exercise which you can use both to try and look at what you need to learn and also to assess what you know. It can therefore be used at any time you like.

If you work in a group, the instruction is for the members of the group to each make a list of all the elements they think are necessary for a process to be described as psychotherapy. Then the group members come together with their lists and make a master list by putting all their ideas together and discussing them and deciding which to throw out and which to keep. You may also do this on your own if you work alone.

What follows is a master list which might have been produced by a group in one of my courses.

1) Psychotherapy requires a minimum of two people: the therapist and the client.

2) Group psychotherapy involves more people, normally between eight and ten and often has two therapists.

3) For work with couples and psychosexual counselling it is usual to have two therapists: one male and one female.

4) The client must have a need which can be met by psychotherapy.

5) Psychotic patients are not usually thought suitable for psychotherapy.

6) The client or patient must want to have psychotherapy.

7) The therapy must take account of projection and transference.

8) The therapy must take account of historical matter as a contributory factor in present behaviour.

9) There must be an implicit or explicit contract between client and therapist as to the nature and duration of the therapy.

10) There must be sufficient time for the sessions and they must go on over a sufficient time span for change to have time to take place.

11) The sessions need to be regular and frequent.

12) In a group there should be established ground rules.

13) Confidentiality must be assured.

14) The therapist must have sufficient training of the right type to be able to carry out the therapy.

15) The therapist must have access to supervision.

16) Where two therapists work together in a group they must have time to think and talk together about the group before and after.

17) The therapist must have a space preferably with a supervisor to look at how his own mental process may be working in the therapy.

ROLE PLAYS

The following role plays can be used to develop understanding of what it feels like to be both client and therapist. There are also opportunities to improve your therapeutic practice.

ROLE PLAY ONE

This role play requires four people.

A therapist. A client. Two observers.

The client works out a problem and a family structure in his own mind. It is then up to the therapist to interview the client and explore the client's problem with him. The job of the observers is to monitor the actions of the therapist in relation to the list of do's and don'ts.

In the first instance, for practice it is better if the client makes the situation fairly simple, but as the role play is repeated, the client may wish to make his situation more complex and to use real life examples which are causing him problems in his work. The role play will work best if the client works out a rough outline of his problem and family situation first and allows himself to develop the scenario spontaneously as he goes along. Feel free to experiment with role play, bearing in mind that its purpose is to give live supervision and practice, so that it should be modified to suit the needs of the group.

ROLE PLAY TWO

This role play requires two people and an audience formed by the remaining group members.

A therapist. A client.

The client works out his situation as above and the aim of the therapist is to try and be "the worst therapist he can possibly imagine".

This is usually very funny and more than one group member should take a turn at taking the role of therapist and client.

CHAPTER SEVEN

WHAT IS PSYCHOTHERAPY

The workshop I give includes a lecture from which the following is taken. In the second edition of the book I have extended this chapter, as the availability of more space allows me to go into much more detail. This factual information is important in trying to assess what psychotherapy is and reflects my own views.

HISTORY

In the last quarter of the 19th century a revolution took place in the way that psychologists viewed mental functioning. It started to become apparent that there were forces at work in the human psyche which we now take for granted and call the unconscious or subconscious. Sigmund Freud has become famous as the person who popularised and codified this notion, but it is important to remember that he was not the only person to be thinking along these lines and that he became the figure head of a movement of ideas which was gaining momentum towards the end of the 19th century. This helps to explain why the ideas of an insignificant Viennese doctor became so influential and powerful world-wide so quickly.

The Interpretation of Dreams, Freud's masterpiece, was remaindered in its first edition and Freud was for many years short of money as he could not attract enough patients for psychoanalysis. However, once his ideas took hold, they spread like wildfire throughout the civilised world.

Freud's writings about the unconscious underpin all later day thinking about psychotherapy. Even the behaviourists acknowledge that unconscious motivations play a part in our behaviour, although they think that attempting to work with the unconscious is a waste of time.

In taking Freud as the basis for our thinking about the unconscious, it is important to distinguish between the thinker and the practitioner. I can not think of any model of psychotherapy which does not acknowledge its debt to

Freud, but only the psychoanalysts still follow his ideas without modification. Many schools of psychotherapy, for example the humanistic school, differ from him widely in both theory and practice. The importance of Freud lies in the way that he made available ideas about the unconscious and emphasised how repressed material affected us in our daily lives, often without our being aware of it.

Freud viewed the mind as being like an iceberg: six seventh of it are submerged and invisible, while the other seventh is visible above the surface. Freud likened the unconscious mind to the submerged six sevenths and the conscious mind to the visible seventh. Jung took this idea further, saying that only a portion of the six sevenths was accessible to the conscious mind and this he called the subconscious.

According to Freud we never forget anything and material we think we have forgotten is held in the unconscious, where it can only be recalled by special techniques such as hypnosis. Freud started off using hypnosis and later free association to gain access to repressed material. Other therapists have developed different and often more direct techniques for accessing subconscious material.

Freud came to his conclusions by working with patients who had hysterical symptoms such as hysterical paralysis (paralysis which had no known physical cause). He discovered that if he hypnotised the patients he was able to help them to remember incidents which they had completely forgotten and which had caused them to develop their hysterical symptoms. He found that this process of recall under hypnosis could cure the hysterical symptoms. Freud discovered that the patient under hypnosis recalled events which he had repressed in childhood, either because they were too painful to recall or because of the guilt associated with them. At the same time Freud came to realise that many of his hysterical patients had been sexually assaulted by their parents. This he called the seduction theory which unfortunately he abandoned in preference for the theory that these people had fantasised their seduction. In so doing he held back the knowledge which has recently come to light about the prevalence of child sexual abuse within the family. John Southgate writes about this in the *Journal of Self-Analysis*, Vol. I.1, and Jeffrey Masson in *Assault on the Truth*.

Freud became dissatisfied with the results he achieved through hypnosis, partly because he was not a good hypnotist and partly because he could not handle the romantic attachments which his young hysterical patients seemed to form with him. He therefore developed the technique known as free association through which he was able to get to unconscious material while at the same time being protected from the romantic projections of his patients. His development of the concept of transference and his technique of interpreting the transference made feelings which the patient had about the analyst a part of the treatment and not something to be acted upon. Descriptions of psychoanalysis and other therapies are to be found in the next chapter.

Jung, after a period of deep and intense friendship with Freud, broke away from him to develop his own ideas and his own methodology. Although his techniques and ideas differed from Freud's, his aim was similar: to make a person consciously aware of the historical reasons for his present behaviour and to help the person become released from the grip that the past holds on the present. In other words, to help a person towards being autonomous in his thoughts, actions and deeds. This I assume, is the aim of all psychotherapy.

Wilhelm Reich, like Jung, had been a leading light in Freud's circle and was rejected by Freud when his ideas no longer concurred with Freud's. Undaunted by his rejection by Freud, Reich went on to develop a body of theory and practice which is vitally important to modern psychotherapy, both analytic and non analytic. He was responsible for developing a method of training psychotherapists, namely the training analysis, which is still the model used today and his early writings made important contributions to psychoanalysis and social thought. He is, however, most importantly remembered for his ideas on the relationship of the body to psychological problems and his ideas underpin most of the modern body orientated therapies. The two most interesting books on Reich are by Sharaf and Boadella.

However, not all psychotherapies have been developed by members of the psychoanalytic movement. The humanistic psychology movement, sometimes referred to as the Third Force, after the Analytic and the Behavioural schools, differs fundamentally from Freud, because it takes an intrinsically hopeful view of the human being and also because it does not follow the medical model of patient and doctor, illness and cure. Humanistic psychology was unified in the 1940's and 1950's by people like Abraham Maslow, who coined the term Third Force, Carl Rogers who developed the client centred approach and Fritz Perls with Gestalt Therapy. In the 1970's the movement consolidated after a period of fast growth, becoming a serious force to be reckoned with in the 1980's.

In the 1920's and 30's J.L. Moreno developed psychodrama, an action based psychotherapy, further developed by his wife Zerka in the 1950's and 60's. Psychodrama is a psychotherapy in which the acting out of past events and the cathartic re-experience of painful emotion is of primary importance. Moreno's approach was "Don't tell me show me" and his work has been very important for the humanistic psychology movement, because he invented most of the techniques which have been developed in Gestalt, Encounter and Primal Therapy.

Reich's ideas have also contributed to the humanistic psychology movement. In the 1930's Reich worked consistently on the idea that we not only repress ideas psychologically but hold these repressed ideas in our bodies in muscles and joints. Reich was interested in energy flow and he believed that this holding or "armouring" restricted and blocked the flow of energy in the human being. He therefore developed methods of psychotherapy in which breathing and touch were used to release this energy and aid the recall of repressed events and emotions. Today Reich's ideas are commonly met in the body orientated therapies such as bioenergetics and primal reintegration.

Behavioural and cognitive psychotherapy are not dealt with here as I do not consider them to be psychotherapies at all, but I am indebted to John Rowan for suggesting that I include E. Lakin Phillips' book in the bibliography as a signpost to those interested in following up behavioural approaches.

WHAT MAKES PSYCHOTHERAPY NECESSARY?

It is perhaps worth reminding you at this stage that far more educated and intelligent people than I have tried to answer this question without success (see Sue Walrond-Skinner, *Dictionary of Psychotherapy*, pp 280 - 281). What I have been trying to do in this book is work towards identifying some common themes which make it easier to define what sorts of practices masquerade as psychotherapy and to identify charlatans. This should help those in the helping professions to know what they are doing, help interested parties to get proper training and help clients in need to find what they are looking for.

Psychotherapy is a process of therapy for the psyche which is consciously undertaken between at least two people, one of whom is nominated the therapist and who is specially trained for the task. The express intention of this therapy is to make a conscious link between the unconscious and conscious minds in order to increase awareness of the historic causes of present psychological symptoms. In some forms of therapy a third element, the body, is linked to the mind, on the basis that old emotional hurts are stored physically in the body. Psychotherapy assumes that there is a separation in the mind between the conscious and the unconscious and that the unconscious contains material and motivations that our conscious mind is unaware of. The aim of psychotherapy is to help the conscious mind to become aware of what is going on in the unconscious. The unconscious mind, although we are unaware of its contents and activity, can affect the conscious mind through affecting the way we think, feel and act.

When a human being is born, he is totally vulnerable and dependent on adults for all his needs in life and continues in this vulnerable state for some years. It seems that in the same way that the physical body is able to protect itself from damage and can repair damage where it occurs, the mind also has its own protective mechanisms which prevent it from being irreversibly damaged. The mind represses emotional material which it can not bear to assimilate and consigns it to the unconscious. It is as if the child says: "I just don't want to know that, so I will forget it." However, this material is not lost altogether, but stored in the unconscious where it is safely out of the way, but can still have its effect on the conscious mind. Providing there is not too much painful material stored in the unconscious, the person can cope with it, but if the unconscious becomes overloaded, symptoms of this overload may push themselves into consciousness and cause the person to seek or be advised to seek help. The symptoms may express themselves as a vague dissatisfaction with life or as specific dissatisfactions, like a failure to make satisfactory relationships or as psychiatric symptoms like depression, a nervous breakdown or psychosis.

The explanation of mental functioning I have just outlined is of course a metaphor, which we use to try and explain what is going on. There is no specific physical place in the body where unconscious repressed material can be stored. It is, as it were, stored either in memory or in the whole body. Repressed material is not like a swelling or a cancer and can therefore not be removed by physical means, whether they be surgery, electric shock or the currently favourite drugs.

An alternative and complementary theory suggests that the individual develops a life style and life strategies which prevent him having to come into contact with situations which affect his ability to keep repressed material in its place. This is closer to the systemic approach to understanding human functioning and can be followed up in the work of Gregory Bateson and Jay Haley. The individual chooses his job and friends and even his marriage partner to suit the needs of the life strategies he has developed, because they work for him in keeping difficult feelings under control. It is only when circumstances such as a death in the family or bad choices such as a change in a job make it impossible for these strategies to continue that symptoms may start to appear. I have explained this further in my tape and booklet on Family Therapy.

WHAT HAPPENS IN PSYCHOTHERAPY?

Initially the therapist will engage in conversation or activity with the client aimed at trying to uncover the unconscious repressed material. Some therapists speak more than others, but mainly it is the therapist's task to listen and use his techniques and skills to help the client uncover the unconscious material himself. In the early stages of the therapy the therapist will educate the client in the therapeutic process and gradually, as confidence builds up between client and therapist, the client will feel able to reveal more of his innermost feelings. The bringing of this material into consciousness is usually accompanied by powerful and often confusing emotions. The client, in order to cope with these emotions will try and blame them onto other people and it is the therapist's job to bring the client back to his own feelings and responsibility for himself. After all, the unreasonable boss or cruel parent is not in the therapy room.

After a while these feelings will start to be directed to the therapist. This process is known as transference and occurs in all psychotherapeutic processes, although different methods rate its importance from very high to very low. The feelings which the client transfers onto the therapist are most likely to reflect the client's repressed feelings towards his parents. At this point pain and the associated guilt make it far too painful for the client to own these feelings for himself. It is therefore easier to rationalise them as being feelings about the therapist and project them onto the therapist.

Differing schools of therapy attach different values to the transference but what cannot be denied is that the transference occurs and that the transferred feelings have a meaning. Nor can it be denied that the therapist himself is subject to these projections which, when they appear in the therapist, are called counter transference. Used carefully to understand his own behaviour through the effect he has on the client, the counter transference can be a very effective tool in therapy.

The therapist has to develop the client's insight into the transferred feelings and help the client to acknowledge, that they are of more significance when they are seen as related not to the therapist, but to the client's feelings about himself, his past life and most probably his parents.

The power and often the inaccuracy of the feelings transferred onto the therapist should alert the therapist to the fact that this is the unconscious showing itself and that communication between client and therapist is no longer taking place on a conscious level. The client is now expressing himself both consciously and unconsciously and this allows the unconscious to receive its therapy for the psyche. By not rejecting the client for having these powerful and unacceptable emotions, the therapist demonstrates to the client that his feelings are acceptable and that he is still acceptable for having them. A common fear in therapy is:" My therapist will only accept me as long as he doesn't know about my terrible fantasies and secrets." The therapist may try to reassure the client, but for the client this reassurance is hollow because he may feel that the therapist is only saying that to make him feel better, or to make him say more than he wants to. Eventually the only reassurance the client can get is to take his courage in both hands and test the therapist out. It is then up to the therapist to demonstrate that these emotions and fantasies are understandable and acceptable and that while they may feel very strong to the client, they do not have the power to destroy the therapist or to cause the therapist to reject him. Melanie Klein is very good at explaining why the client feels that these feelings will destroy either himself or the therapist or both of them. Klein does this by relating them back to the period of babyhood when the baby does feel enormously powerful and has very violent feelings which it fears could destroy the mother and/or itself.

In behaving in an accepting and caring way the therapist fulfils the unfulfilled needs of the child which the client's parents were not able to do and the client is therefore able to start to behave in the present, free from the effect of the emotions and events which happened in the past. In this sense psychotherapy can be said to heal past hurts and to allow a person to gain true autonomy in the present. At its best psychotherapy is a healing process for the psyche, not an embarrassing or critical evaluation of a person's most secret and delicate feelings.

The sheer quantity of reorganisation and the extreme quality of the emotions involved accounts for the fact that it takes quite a length of time, anything from about a year to ten years, for real change to come about. Three years is a sensible average.

The length of time involved often puts people off embarking on therapy and many people have searched for ways of shortening the process with little success. Today the commitment of time and money is shorter than the one hour a day, five days a week, forty eight weeks of the year over several years of classic psychoanalysis, which Freud's original patients undertook. Most people go for therapy once or twice a week and the techniques of humanistic psychology have helped to speed up the process, but there is still no instant cure nor in terms of psychotherapy is it likely that there ever will be.

However, it must be remembered and emphasised, that problems do not just go away and that when psychotherapy is successful it can make all the time, money, effort, and pain of therapy supremely worthwhile.

AN IMPORTANT NOTE ON FEMINIST PSYCHOTHERAPY

The role of the women's movement in criticising the underlying sexist assumptions inherent in much psychotherapy has been vital in bringing about changes in how psychotherapy is practised and I felt it therefore important to give it a section of its own under the heading 'What is Psychotherapy', as more and more a feminist perspective is changing our understanding of psychotherapy.

Many of the criticisms of psychotherapy which have been voiced in recent times are to do with its paternalism. Most of the innovators in the field of therapy were men who were anxious to help their clients to conform to an existing and patriarchal social order. As the social order has changed and the change in the position of women in our society has been one of greatest of these changes, so women and men have become dissatisfied with a psychotherapy which does not take account of these changes. Feminist psychotherapists are women, often with a conventional psychotherapy training, who have identified sexist trends inherent in psychotherapy and attempt to conduct their therapeutic relationship with their clients in a way which respects them both as women and as clients. So, for example if a woman speaks of her problems in relation to food, the therapist is as likely to help the client to understand these problems in relationship to the values placed on thinness in our society as much as to the client's own personal history. For example, anorexia may be viewed as a response to a male dominated society which views how you look as being more important than who you are. This is obviously an important enhancement to an understanding of psychological problems, because it forces the therapist to relate to the cultural context of the client as well as to the individual's own history.

The feminist therapist is someone whose consciousness of women's issues has been raised. She recognises that men have dominated women for too long and is helping her clients to redress the balance. Some therapists take a very hard line on feminist issues and others are more liberal, but they all share a rejection of male domination in our society. This means that the therapist no longer accepts male values as "correct values" and will, where appropriate, help the client to see that it may be important to change how she views herself in society in order to resolve difficulties in her past.

In practice all feminist therapists are women because they believe that it is only possible for women to escape the effect of millennia of male domination by working together as women. In fact many hard line feminists are against women having male therapists. For this reason it is a moot point whether it is possible for there to be such a thing as a male feminist therapist.

One of the hallmarks of the women's movement has been women doing things for themselves using self help groups. Women's therapy has been no exception, so that self help therapy groups have grown in which women run a therapy group with members of the group taking responsibility for facilitating according to their ability to be helpful at any given moment. This process is vividly described in Ernst and Goodison's *In Our Own Hands*.

The people most responsible for the development of feminist therapy in Britain were Luise Eichenbaum and Susie Orbach who founded the Women's Therapy Centre in 1976 in London which is still going strong and which provides all sorts of feminist therapy, both individual and group (see address list).

Evidently this chapter has only skimmed the surface of the subject 'What is Psychotherapy'. In it I have tried to describe the historical roots of psychotherapy and show some elements which I view as essential components of a psychotherapeutic process. A further review of the main types of psychotherapy available in Britain makes up the next chapter.

CHAPTER EIGHT

TYPES OF PSYCHOTHERAPY: INDIVIDUAL

There are dozens of different types of psychotherapy, some very similar to each other, while others have very marked differences of philosophy and technique. In this chapter and the next, the major schools are outlined without making an attempt to be comprehensive, which would be outside the scope of this book. I have attempted to say something about the major schools of psychotherapy and why I think others are not really psychotherapies or are confused in their thinking. The section attempts to fill gaps in the reader's knowledge with information which I think is important to anyone trying to decide what psychotherapy is. I hope that it will also serve to clear up misconceptions. The book list and address list are there to facilitate further research. Readers wanting to know more about the individual therapies should consult the reading list bearing in mind especially the *Psychotherapy Handbooks* series (Open University Press) edited by Windy Dryden and the ... *in action* series (SAGE Publications), also edited by Windy Dryden. For information about therapy and training consult the address list.

There are three major influences on the development of psychotherapy. These are Freud and the psychodynamic movement, the humanistic psychology movement and the Behavioural Cognitive School. I have written at length about the Psychodynamic Schools and about humanistic psychology which fall into the definition of psychotherapy I have been working towards in this book and have paid only scant attention to the behavioural and cognitive models because, while they may be effective, as their practitioners claim, I feel they fall outside our definition of psychotherapy.

Whether psychotherapy is helpful in the treatment of mental illness (for a discussion of this term see Chapter Ten) is a matter of hotly contested debate between psychiatrists, psychoanalysts, psychotherapists and those who favour behavioural, cognitive or physical treatments. Bruno Bettelheim, in his very interesting book *Freud and Man's Soul* asserts that Freud never intended psychoanalysis as a cure for mental illness and Anthony Clare, Professor of Psychiatry at the University of London, holds psychotherapy in low esteem as a treatment. However, in my own clinical practice I have found that psychotherapy can help mental patients, many of whom favour it themselves over physical treatments. I have found that the action therapies used within a humanistic psychology group approach are most beneficial for mental patients and perhaps this stems from the fact that Moreno developed psychodrama specifically for use in psychiatry.

PSYCHODYNAMIC THERAPIES

The therapies which have developed from the writings of Freud are usually referred to under the portmanteau term of psychoanalysis, which in Britain has developed Freud's ideas under the influence of D.W. Winnicott, W.R. Bion and Melanie Klein among others. In psychiatry, psychotherapy and psychoanalysis are usually viewed as synonymous and the psychoanalytic movement has been a very powerful influence on the development of psychotherapy in Britain. An influence which I for one do not think is beneficial because of the narrowness of its line of thought.

Also under the heading psychodynamic therapy comes the Analytic Psychology of Jung which he developed in parallel with Freud, when for a period they were close collaborators (1907 - 1913).

Individual Psychology is the form of therapy developed by Alfred Adler, another of Freud's collaborators which is not widely represented in Britain although it has been influential in some educational circles.

PSYCHOANALYSIS

This is the name given to classical Freudian psychotherapy with the client on a couch and is the model of psychotherapy so beloved of cartoonists. Freud developed this form of therapy around the turn of the century after experimenting with hypnosis as a cure for hysteria. The idea of the couch and the darkened room is to simulate as far as possible that time just between wakefulness and sleep when a person is neither awake nor asleep and images pop into the mind without conscious control. Also the couch with the patient lying prone is supposed to allow and encourage the patient into a regressed state, such as was experienced in an earlier stage of childhood. The therapist sits out of the patient's sight line, so that the patient is not affected by the therapist's responses and can say whatever he likes without fear of censure. At the same time, because he cannot see the therapist's reactions, he can form his own fantasies about the therapist. These fantasies can be used as a rich field for interpretation of the patient's neurosis. For example, if a patient says to the therapist "...and I know that you are angry about that", the therapist can interpret back: "It is not me who is angry, but perhaps you think I must be angry with you just like your father was." From here the patient can go on to explore his feelings about his father.

In this form of psychotherapy the analyst gives no instruction to the patient as to what to talk about, apart from expressing an interest in the patient's dreams. The patient is instructed to talk of whatever comes into his head, no matter how embarrassing or odd it may seem and to continue to talk of the spontaneous images which come into the mind without censoring anything. For obvious reasons this process is called Free Association and this is the mainstay of psychoanalysis. The analyst attempts to interpret these images in a way which helps the client to understand his own mental functioning. It is this interpretation which is claimed to be the curative element in psychoanalysis. Interpretation allows the bringing to consciousness of repressed material which allows the patient to be freed from the associated guilt.

As the process of revelation and interpretation continues, the patient starts to have fantasies about the analyst, called projections, until a full blown transference neurosis is formed and it is the final interpretation of this transference neurosis which brings about the cure.

This in a nutshell is Freudian psychoanalysis and there are still plenty of analysts who practice in this very rigid way. However, there are many analysts who have developed Freud's methods and his ideas so that not all psychoanalysts use the couch and the darkened room. Many Freudians, while still thinking of themselves as analytically based, do not call themselves psychoanalysts.

Psychoanalysis is basically an individual therapy although there is such a thing as psychoanalytic group therapy. Patients are encouraged to have as many as five fifty minute sessions a week over several years. It is therefore very expensive and is not usually available on the N.H.S. except through the Tavistock Clinic in London and a few other similar centres.

Analytic psychotherapy does not demand such a heavy commitment with the number of sessions being normally one or two per week.

Membership of the British Psychoanalytic Society requires a personal psychoanalysis as the main plank of training and supervised practice before and after acceptance.

KLEINIAN ANALYSIS

One of the most important developments of Freudian theory and practice was undertaken by Melanie Klein who lived in England in the 1930's. Freud's insights into psychotherapy led him to analyse the patient as far back as infancy, but Melanie Klein went further back into the patient's life, right into babyhood. This, she claimed, produced a far deeper and more thorough analysis. Melanie Klein's influence was and still is very strong in British psychoanalytic circles.

OBJECT RELATIONS

A reviewer rightly objected to the omission of this part of Psychoanalysis in previous editions. The Object Relations school is associated with the names of Robert Fairbairn, Harry Guntrip, Donald Winnicott and Michael Balint in this country, and Otto Kernberg in the USA.

Object relations theory places emphasis all the time on the objects outside of the individual, which may be a person or a part of a person, rather than on the instincts inside the person. These objects and part objects can be internalised and become internal objects. So we may have inside us all sorts of internalised people and parts of people, which we relate to in fantasy and on an emotional level.

There is a lot of emphasis in object relations theory on the relationship between the baby, in the first hours, days and weeks of life, and its mother. Some go so far as to say that there is no such thing as an isolated baby, and that it studied. Hence among the practitioners of this form of therapy there is a lot of emphasis on the transference, as representing in the here-and-now the mother-baby relationship as it was at the beginning. This emphasis on people in relationships is of course very acceptable to feminists, and much of the work of the Women's Therapy Centre is based on object relations theory.

Object relations theory is influential not only in psychoanalysis, but also in many other forms of psychotherapy.

JUNGIAN ANALYSIS

Jung was developing his ideas on the unconscious and psychotherapy at about the same time as Freud, but in Switzerland. He corresponded with Freud and they became very firm colleagues and, after meeting, close friends. However, their friendship foundered after a few years on doctrinal and personal grounds. The reasons have been the subject of lengthy conjecture and analysis ever since.

Jungian analysis does not use the couch nor does it employ the technique of free association. It still shares with psychoanalysis an interest in the unconscious and a model of psychotherapy which says that repressed material can be released through interpretation. In Jungian analysis however, it is the image itself which is interpreted and not the patient's associations with the image. A Jungian might ask a person who has dreamt about a room: What does that room mean to you? whereas a Freudian might ask the question: If you lie back and relax, what images come into your mind when you think of that room?

Jung's interest in the analysing of the image itself came from his discovery of what he called the Collective Unconscious. By studying other cultures Jung realised that certain images, such as for example the earth mother or the devil, the river and the mountain, occurred in the mythology of all cultures and in the dreams of the people who lived in those cultures. He therefore claimed that these images were universal and because they occurred in all cultures were in fact part of the human make up and not culturally determined. Someone who had never seen an umbrella would not dream of one, and therefore he might not have the Mary Poppins idea of being able to fly on a wind blown umbrella, but people in all cultures dreamt of birds and flying like a bird or being flown off with by a bird.

Jung went on to suggest that these common images had common meanings, which he called archetypes, which could be used in the analysis of dreams. Jung also encouraged his patients to paint and draw and write poetry, all of which are thought to be appropriate material for the session and for analysis.

Jung was interested in the self which could be realised through therapy and which would allow each person to become what he really had the potential to be. This process he called self actualisation. Similarly he laid emphasis on the importance of the shadow, that is to say the negative part of the self and its importance in the development of the soul and the self. This is seen by Jungians as a far more wide ranging and integrated view of the individual than Freud's emphasis on sexuality.

Jung laid down no hard and fast rules as to how therapy should be conducted, but it is normal for the patient and the therapist to sit face to face and for material brought to the session to be analysed. The material can be feelings about people outside as well as feelings about the therapist, so that transference is an integral part of the process. Indeed, Jungians also bring in the therapist's countertransference on to the patient. An integral part of the process is dream analysis and analysis of the patient's art work if there is any. Jungian Therapy usually involves two or three sessions a week and there are Jungians working in the N.H.S., but not many. Jung has however been quite influential on many of the therapies which use the creative arts, especially art therapy which is available on the N.H.S. Training involves a lengthy personal analysis and supervised practice and there is active accreditation and training of Jungian analysts in Britain.

ARCHETYPAL PSYCHOLOGY

This form of therapy has been developed by the Jungian intellectual James Hillman. I have referred in my *Therapist's Bibliography* to the difficulties that I have had in reading his work, but as far as I can understand it, his work does not so much analyse the archetype, but attempts to get the patient to interact with and confront the reality in himself of the archetypal material he brings to the sessions. The therapy takes the archetype as a reality for the patient and not as something which stands in the place of the patient's reality. Hillman places emphasis on the imaginal aspect of the human psyche and emphasises the importance of the imagination in creating the psyche so that he views the enlarging of the soul as more important than an analysis of the psyche which is by definition reductionist.

There are not many archetypal psychotherapists in Britain although many therapists, especially Jungians, will have read and been influenced by Hillman's work. Although I am not personally impressed by Hillman, many people find his work extremely important and an address for further information and training is included in the address list.

HUMANISTIC PSYCHOLOGY

There are many humanistic psychologists who work individually with clients, but the majority of their techniques are developed from approaches which are group therapies. I have dealt with each approach under the heading of group therapy. There are also people whose techniques and orientation in individual therapy are Freudian or Jungian but who have adapted these approaches to fit within a humanistic framework.

The main aspect of humanistic psychology, which marks it out from other forms of therapy, is that it adopts a model which sees the human being as being basically "all right". Events which happen to the individual and things which are done to him are seen as causing psychological problems. Humanistic psychology does not see the human being as being engaged in a struggle to come to terms with a basically flawed human situation in which the strict and critical Super Ego is engaged in an endless battle with the hedonistic and uncontrolled id, as Freudian psychology describes the human predicament. It therefore seeks to enhance the joyfulness of human life and to encourage people to realise their own individual potential. Self realisation and development of the real self are its watch words. It has the advantage of being able to help people to change troublesome symptomology much more quickly than psychodynamic methods and practitioners generally conform to our definition of what is needed to be a psychotherapist.

Humanistic psychology has drawn on many different thinkers in its development. Freud with his emphasis on the unconscious and the part that unconscious motivation plays in our everyday life is the first important influence. Techniques in humanistic psychology stem from Moreno with his emphasis on action and Reich with his emphasis on the body. Philosophically Perls has been influential with his emphasis on personal responsibility as has Rogers with his development of the person centred approach.

There has been a great contribution from Eastern philosophy with its emphasis on a holistic approach to life in which psychology and spirituality mingle together rather than being split off from each other. Ken Wilber's work has been of great significance here. Other writers such as Mahrer and Maslow have contributed greatly to the bringing together of humanistic psychology ideas and unifying them into a definable body of psychology.

One of the most important aspects of humanistic psychology is its emphasis on spirituality. Humanistic psychology allies itself with no religion per se but recognises that human beings have a spiritual side which they can benefit from developing.

The phrase I have used earlier, " which they can benefit from developing" tells us a lot about the humanistic psychology model, because it does not tell people what they ought to do, but invites them to investigate their own possibilities for health, healing and growth, and to incorporate those which are right for them into their own life.

The spirit of trying to find out what is right for me is more important than adherence to any particular school or method. Indeed, there is scope within the humanistic model for experimentation with different methods of psychotherapy through which the individual finds out the best model for him at that particular time on his journey through life. This model is very different from the medical model of illness and cure used in the psychodynamic therapies and in it mistakes and failures are given equal importance alongside successes as being aids to a person's learning how to live. It may seem paradoxical that the therapies which have come about through a reaction against the medical model should be so successful in treating the sort of problems which are called mental illnesses by doctors. Techniques drawn from Psychodrama, Gestalt and Encounter are used in some mental hospitals in Britain with often very good effect. Outside of hospitals many people with quite severe chronic conditions report very good and lasting results after quite short experiences of humanistic psychology methods.

Humanistic psychology concerns itself with all areas of human life and sees itself not only as a model for alleviating suffering, but also as a channel for human growth and is the philosophy behind the growth movement. This accounts for the eclecticism of humanistic psychology which is only too willing to explore and incorporate any philosophy or technique which helps to develop the enhancement of human potential. To some this makes it seem like a magpie philosophy which seizes on any shiny new idea. In fact, the central core of its ideology which puts people first, makes for a very strong and vibrant movement, able to incorporate new ideas without being overwhelmed by them.

BEHAVIOURAL AND COGNITIVE PSYCHOTHERAPY

These methods are increasing in popularity in Britain today, especially among clinical psychologists working in the N.H.S. and in private practice. Many claims are made for their efficacy and I have no reason to want to dispute them, but this does not mean that they are psychotherapies in the sense that we have been working towards in this book. They do not attempt to uncover repressed material, nor do they try to get back to past painful experiences. In fact, many behaviourists view attempts to uncover past material as an irrelevant task.

The work of these therapists is firmly placed in the present. It attempts to help people to change through examining their present behaviour to changing it either by viewing it differently or by searching for more rewarding forms of behaviour.

There is no need in this form of therapy for the therapist to have had therapy himself and there is no place in it for a consideration of transference and projection, either on the part of the client or the therapist.

It is up to these therapies to justify themselves in their own way and develop their own terminology which suits their own form of work. It is a contradiction in terms for them to call themselves psychotherapies as much as it would be for the brain surgeon carrying out frontal lobotomies to call himself a psychotherapist.

CHAPTER NINE

TYPES OF PSYCHOTHERAPY: GROUPS

GROUP PSYCHOTHERAPY AND GROUP THERAPY

The use of groups is gaining in popularity in psychiatry, social work and education all the time. The majority of these groups can not be described as psychotherapy groups, because they do not meet our criteria for what constitutes psychotherapy. Often group therapy occupies itself with activities which, because they are carried on in a group, allow members to receive support and feed back from each other as well as achieving economies of scale. However desirable this may be, there is no way in which a social skills group or a cookery group or a mutual support group can be thought of as group psychotherapy.

The therapy group in which people talk about their problems and share their experiences with others may also be very helpful to people with emotional problems, on the basis that a trouble shared is a trouble halved and that confession is good for the soul. However, such a group can only be described as psychotherapy if it is organised in a way which fits our criteria.

It is often stated that group psychotherapy should not be individual therapy undertaken in a group. Some of the group therapies described here may seem to include individual therapy taking place in a group, for example psychodrama, but these therapies involve the emotions of the "watchers" very powerfully and therefore can claim to be group therapy for all their members.

TALKING GROUP PSYCHOTHERAPY

This could be said to be a portmanteau term for any group which meets regularly under the auspices of one or more leaders who are trained in psychotherapy. The structure of these groups is similar, in that people sit in a circle and talk or remain silent depending on their emotional state at the time. The therapist takes the role of organiser, setting the time and space for the group meetings and interpreting or commenting upon what is said and done in the group.

This sort of therapy usually takes place in small groups of between eight and ten people, but also in large groups often called community meetings. If the aim of the community meeting is to organise practical matters, it may well be that it is therapeutic, but it is not psychotherapy. In therapeutic communities the community meeting is seen as an essential part of the overall therapy.

Psychotherapy groups can be open or closed and ongoing or of limited duration and the tools used by the therapist will vary. Usually they are the interpretation of repressed material and dreams and the working through of transference. Group members receive support and feedback from each other. A good group therapist can facilitate the expression of very powerful emotions by group members and the resolution of deep seated emotional problems. However, the method is not generally as effective as action methods. This sort of therapy is occasionally available on the N.H.S.

THE TAVISTOCK GROUP

The most influential thinker and therapist in British group psychotherapy was W.R. Bion, who started what is commonly known as the Tavistock Group. Sessions have often been described to me as the sort of group "where everybody just sits for fifty minutes and nobody says anything." Bion had very specific reasons for conducting the group in this way and very specific structures for interpreting group work behaviour, which are outlined in his book *Experiences in Groups*. Bion's work has been of major importance in developing our understanding of how group dynamics operate, but his therapy group, while it fulfilled the main criteria of a psychotherapy group, seems to have been of little help to patients and even harmful to some of them, as Yalom points out in his book *Group Therapy*. The Tavistock Group is still seen as having a vital part to play in the training of group therapists.

THE GROUP ANALYTIC MOVEMENT

The Institute of Group Analysis is a large and influential organisation for the teaching of group therapy and the treatment of patients through the group analytic method. The Institute developed out of the work of people like Foulkes and Anthony and Robin Skynner was an influential founder member.

The Group Analytic Approach involves one therapist in a small group of approximately eight or ten people meeting regularly at a fixed time over a fixed number of weeks. The therapist assumes a low profile and offers himself as a blank screen to the group in which he interprets individual and group behaviour as he feels appropriate. The interpretations and apparent detachment of the therapist are often instrumental in uncovering repressed material and creating both individual and group transference on to the leader and other group members. Feedback is seen as an important learning tool and the process of interpretation by the therapist, as well as confrontation by other group members, are important forms of feedback. Often very powerful and deeply felt emotions are resolved through this method.

In the training offered by the Institute there are also opportunities to study large group processes. Training, training therapy and supervision are all treated very seriously by the Institute.

My own experience of this method leads me to believe that it is not as effective as humanistic group work techniques as a therapeutic tool, although it is very useful as a teaching method. This is mainly because the method seems to work best for people who have a good understanding of its theoretical basis and are strong enough to not be frightened of the very strong emotions it can evoke.

HUMANISTIC PSYCHOLOGY

I have left the most important of the group therapies till last, because the Humanistic approach has given rise to a large number of group therapies, all of which require a short description. I have chosen to give a good deal of space to humanistic psychology because of its importance in psychotherapy and because it is generally under-represented in courses on psychology. Humanistic psychology is no longer a peripheral activity and with the number of training programmes now in operation and the increased number of therapists being trained, the movement is proving that it has a lot to offer and has to be taken seriously.

Humanistic psychology is the most accessible and effective of the group therapies in helping both those people with problems and the mentally ill. It is also probably the most misunderstood and abused of the therapies.

Humanistic psychology is also a method of personal growth. It was taken up by many ill trained and ill equipped people in the sixties and early seventies and this led to many unfortunate experiences, and has given it a bad name in some circles. However, the movement in Britain has now pulled itself together and is properly organised with a central organisation, the Association of Humanistic Psychology in Britain with a practitioners group, the Association of Humanistic Psychology Practitioners, which demands and maintains a very high level of professional standards. The Practitioners Group is actively represented in the United Kingdom Standing Conference for Psychotherapy.

Today many occupational therapists, nurses, social workers, teachers and even psychologists and psychiatrists have become qualified practitioners and use their knowledge to great effect in their work.

The humanistic psychology model does not follow the medical idea of a sick patient who will be cured by a knowledgeable and powerful doctor. The model used is essentially democratic in that the person coming for help, usually known as the client, and the therapist are involved in a co-operative quest towards health and growth. The client is therefore viewed as having to take responsibility for his own health and has much more power in the relationship. This of course makes it seem threatening to those practitioners who are not secure enough in their own therapeutic orientation to be able to take criticism from their clients and patients.

Humanistic psychology has drawn on many different thinkers in its development. Freud with his emphasis on the unconscious and the part that unconscious motivation plays in our everyday life is an important influence, although the humanistic model of psychic disturbance is a direct reaction against Freud's deterministic and essentially dismal view of the human condition. The action therapists, the first of whom was Moreno, have been instrumental in developing a large number of techniques used in humanistic psychology and many of these have been developed by Perls in Gestalt Therapy. Thirdly, Wilhelm Reich has been an important influence with his emphasis on the body in therapy. After all, if your feelings aren't in your body, where the hell are they?

The philosophical basis of humanistic psychology is as important as its techniques and thinkers such as Mahrer and Maslow have contributed greatly to the philosophical underpinning of the humanistic model. They have placed emphasis on the perfectibility of the human being and seen that psychology has to be holistic in the sense that it must involve itself as much with body and spirit as the mind. In the humanistic model we all have the potential for growth as well as the potential for madness and decline.

HUMANISTIC GROUP PSYCHOTHERAPIES

As I have already said, humanistic psychology is concerned with growth as much as with therapy and it is often possible to attend humanistic groups for an afternoon, a weekend or a week. You can even combine it with a holiday such as at the growth centre on the Greek island of Skyros. This does not mean that you can achieve psychotherapy in a weekend, although there are people who go to a group to work on a certain problem or find the activity of going to several different groups therapeutic. The leaders of these groups will in their training have been expected to be in continuous therapy over a long period of time, whether in a group, individually, or both and also to have regular supervision. It therefore follows, that in the main humanistic psychologists recommend, that a person wishing to undertake humanistic psychotherapy should commit himself to a regular group or individual programme of therapy.

PSYCHODRAMA

Psychodrama, developed and pioneered by Jacob Moreno and later by his wife Zerka, was the first humanistic group therapy and most of the later techniques used in humanistic therapy were first used and documented by Moreno.

Moreno was a contemporary of Freud's in Vienna, but reacted strongly to Freud's determinism and the lack of spontaneity and creativity in his work. Moreno was interested in change, both in the individual and in the world and recognised that through dramatic action related to the client's own problems such change could come about in everyday life. According to Moreno the two most important elements in human life are spontaneity and role playing, which he viewed as methods of confronting and resolving problems. He decided in the 1920's that if his ideas were to gain wider recognition, he would have to leave Vienna for the United States, where after a very hard struggle his work is now widely recognised and freely available in most major cities and psychiatric hospitals. Psychodrama has in recent years been gaining ground in England too: there are now several established centres in England of which Holwell in Devon was the first and is now the most influential. Psychodrama has been very successful in helping people in mental hospitals which must owe a lot to the fact that Moreno developed his work along clinical lines as a way of helping the mentally ill. Some psychodrama is practised in the N.H.S.

Moreno's main work was developing a group therapy called psychodrama in which an individual (known as the protagonist) can work on a past, present or future problem by acting it out with the help of a therapist (known as a director) and other members of the group (known as auxiliary egos). The other group members themselves receive a lot from watching or participating in the protagonist's therapy, but it is the opportunity to have one's own psychodrama which is the central therapeutic moment. At first Moreno used specially trained helpers to play the parts of the auxiliary egos, but came to recognise that members of the group received a great deal from helping others and that they were better able to facilitate the protagonist than the specially trained helpers.

This democratic approach to therapy is inherent in the terms Director and Protagonist, the idea being that I try to explain my story and put over my side of it to a director, who helps me to act it out therapeutically.

Moreno made two very important contributions in developing the idea of role play and role reversal. Role play allows the protagonist to act out what happened and to enact what happened again and again if necessary. Role play also allows the protagonist to change history and try out "what if's" and see what they feel like. It gives the protagonist the opportunity to enact scenes, which he wanted to enact, but was never able to, for whatever reason and to enact scenes the way he would have liked them to happen. This can be very healing.

Role reversal, in which the protagonist takes the role of the significant other and plays as if he were that person, is a very significant element in psychodrama as it allows the protagonist to see how it feels to be the other person and to explore that person's motivation for doing whatever they did or didn't do to the protagonist.

It is inherent in the psychodramatic model of mental disturbance, that problems arise for the individual because of acts of omission or commission by parents or significant others and the aim of the psychodrama is to bring an awareness of these acts to the forefront of the protagonist's world and to release powerful emotions linked to them and then to repair and heal the old wounds. This powerful and spontaneous overflow of emotion is called a catharsis, usually expressed in screaming or sobbing which, while it may seem very violent at the time, generally leads to the protagonist feeling better afterwards.

Perhaps the most important therapeutic element of the humanistic approach is that it is not afraid of the open expression of powerfully abreacted feeling. This should be compared with the reaction of the doctor in Dialogue 5.

One of the problems encountered by the protagonist in psychodrama is that often the role playing, role reversal and catharsis can get stuck and Moreno developed a number of techniques which he used to overcome this problem and enhance the psychodrama. These are: doubling and the use of the double, empty chair technique, soliloquy, fantasy, physicalising an emotional state, back to back and many others. Some of these have been developed by other therapists and incorporated in different ways into other therapies, notably Gestalt with its use of the hot seat.

The problem for anybody wishing to develop an action therapy is that any technique they can think up was probably used first by Moreno.

Moreno also addressed himself to group issues through what he called sociodrama in which group issues could be played out by all members in the group taking imaginative parts or playing themselves.

Moreno used this technique with families, organisations and even with communities. He even wanted to involve world leaders in psychodramatic contact through which he believed international conflict could be resolved.

It is often asserted by critics of psychodrama that it is merely individual therapy carried on in a group. However, these critics have obviously never been in a psychodrama group because, apart from the benefits for the individuals who are not protagonists that I have already mentioned above, the psychodrama group gives space for the investigation of individual and group transference on to the director as well as using sociodramatic techniques for examining and resolving problems.

I myself have experienced many very powerful feelings within a psychodrama group where I was a member. I have also led groups in which transference and group dynamics have been very successfully resolved through psychodrama and sociodrama. The psychodramatist deals with these elements of group therapy actively and therefore much more directly than can the group analyst.

GESTALT THERAPY

The father of Gestalt therapy, Fritz Perls, was a psychoanalyst who became dissatisfied with the passivity and rigidity of Psychoanalysis and who worked with many other therapists, among them Reich and Moreno, in the search for a better form of therapy. He was influenced by Gestalt Psychology with its emphasis on the need for completion.

The major concern of Gestalt Therapy is the emphasis placed on personal responsibility. If life is not what you want it to be, it is up to you to do something about it. The aim of therapy is to help you to be able to make these changes and lead the life you want. The Gestalt therapist recognises, that people are often blocked by unfinished business (an incomplete Gestalt) and helps them to finish this business by dealing with it in the here and now. Perls placed great emphasis on living in the present. It is for him a fact that a person can only live in the present, not the past or the future. Change therefore only occurs in the present. Therapeutically this means that the Gestalt therapist will often ask the question: What are you feeling now? and find this more important than information about what you felt then. Implicit in this importance laid on personal responsibility and being in the present are the importance of saying "I feel" and "I think" as opposed to "One thinks", "you feel" and making statements, not asking questions. In this way the individual is encouraged to take responsibility for himself in therapy and therefore in his life outside.

The Gestalt therapist uses a lot of techniques such as empty chair and role reversal, developed from psychodrama, but is unlikely to use them in as formal a way as the psychodramatist.

Gestalt is popular in Britain and its popularity is increasing. The techniques are easy for people to understand and use and Gestalt is especially successful with adolescents. The techniques give vent easily to powerful emotions and although most people find this beneficial, some people also find that the emphasis on action detracts from the benefits of being able to reflect upon and think about their problems.

There are established training courses in Britain and practitioners are able to receive supervision, although there is no specific and overall controlling body. The idea of a central control is against the idea of freedom and individual responsibility and while this means there can be bad therapists, it also leads to greater freedom and creativity for others.

Many people working in the N.H.S. and social services are able to offer Gestalt therapy and there are many private practitioners.

PRIMAL THERAPY AND PRIMAL REINTEGRATION

The Primal movement was one of the great innovations of the late 60's, even the Beatles tried primal therapy. The movement, started by Arthur Janov, was perhaps better at self publicity than therapy and many people found themselves disappointed to find that Janov's claim to have discovered "the cure for neurosis" was more than a little exaggerated.

Janov argued (by no means originally, the hypothesis having been developed by Freud and Breuer in the nineteenth century) that neurosis is caused by early childhood trauma: a process of cutting off in early childhood from the pain caused to the infant by parents and others around him. These "primal pains" were so painful to the child, that the child chose to cut off completely from the pain of feeling them. The point at which this cut off was made Janov called the primal scene and the aim of his therapy was to allow the client in fantasy to relive the primal scene so as to release the primal pain, which the client had locked up inside him and which caused his neurotic behaviour. Often this led to a cathartic release, expressed in a scream which Janov used as the title of his first book, *The Primal Scream*.

Janov argued that we develop a series of defences to keep us from feeling primal pain and that these defences have to be broken down before the primal pain can be re-experienced. He had a series of very powerful methods for assisting this break down, including requesting clients to go without sleep, remain isolated, and give up all their primal defences such as drink, T.V. and smoking. This was to precede the three week primal intensive in which the client worked everyday on reliving primal pain with the aid of the primal therapist.

This process led to very powerful regressions and often miraculous relief of symptoms, but more often than not the effects were short lived, sometimes even detrimental, in that people became very fixed in their regressed states and became dependent. These people are sometimes known as primal junkies. Training is rigorous and expensive and there are a few Janov trained therapists in Britain.

PRIMAL INTEGRATION

Bill Swartley and his colleague Diane Dryden brought to England from Canada a more therapeutic form of primal therapy, called Primal Integration, which was pioneered in England by Frank Lake, see his book *Clinical Theology*. Swartley apparently first introduced the term primal integration as a defence against Janov's patenting the term Primal Therapy!

Primal reintegration is a holistic form of therapy involving mind, body and spirit. In this form of therapy much emphasis was placed upon reintegrating the primal experience, because it was recognised that simply re-experiencing the primal pain was not enough and that the important thing was how the individual was able to reintegrate himself after experiencing the release from primal pain.

Primal therapy tends to have slipped into the mists of the past which was the sixties. Bill Swartley is dead, Diane Dryden no longer uses primal work at all and Janov, while still working, is hardly the prominent figure on the scene he once was.

However, the influence of Janov was so strong on many therapists who were working in the late sixties and early seventies that I have felt it important to write about primal therapy, even though any one wanting to experience it might find it difficult to find a therapist in Britain and almost impossible outside of London or on the N.H.S.

ENCOUNTER

I propose a brief overview of the large field of Encounter because, like Primal Therapy, it was more important for its influence than for its presence in England today. The main thing about an encounter group and the encounter movement was the importance that it placed on genuineness and directness of communication between people and specifically between people in a group or therapeutic setting. In an encounter a genuine exchange takes place between two or more people with as many of their masks down as possible. Surprise, surprise: the first person to use the term was Moreno. In 1914 he wrote:

"A meeting of two: eye to eye, face to face. And when you are near I will tear your eyes out and place them instead of mine, and you will tear my eyes out and place them instead of yours. Then I will look at you with your eyes and you will look at me with mine."

The experience of the group is often very powerful, especially when you have never felt anything like it before. Often people complain that it would be impossible to behave like that outside, in their normal lives. However, I believe that much of the increased emotional openness which some people experience in their lives and which is prevalent in our society today as compared with the early sixties is an effect of the thinking inherent in the encounter movement.

THE ENCOUNTER GROUP

In the sort of group run by Carl Rogers the main substrate of the group was talking honestly and openly about yourself and your feelings toward others in the group. However, Will Schutz developed a number of exercises which could be used in the encounter group to enhance such communication. Many of these are developments or direct lifts from Psychodrama and Gestalt.

BODY THERAPY

Before starting on this section I feel that I should declare an interest. I am currently receiving Postural Integration: a form of body therapy which I am finding very helpful and which is enabling me to deal with material I have only touched in 23 years of other forms of therapy.

This in itself is interesting, because much of what I have done up to now involved the body in one way or another. What differentiates the body therapies from other therapies is that they start with the body as a way into the person. I have not chosen to enquire too deeply into the theory behind P.I. while having the therapy, but I can describe what happens.

I take off all my clothes including my watch and lie on a massage table. After some gentle massage the therapist works very deeply and slowly on one part of my body at a time. I am instructed to try and breathe into the pressure point being worked on and to negotiate a level of pain which is acceptable to me and which allows me still to breathe into the area being massaged.

The work has had two effects on me so far. The first is that it has high-lighted the enormous difficulty I have in acknowledging the fallacy in the argu-ment: "It is only helpful if it hurts", which has led to a major re-evaluation of my self punishing behaviour and thinking. The second is that the therapy has formed a very powerful negative transference which I have never experienced so strongly before. This transference has been very helpful to me in sorting out feelings towards my mother and a deep seated Jewish fear of Germans, which I discovered was tied up with a fear and confusion about my mother.

All this may indeed have happened only because I was ready for it, but on the other hand it has happened and happened during P.I.

Wilhelm Reich is the starting point of any writing about body work. Although there are many different approaches to body work, they all have important common points and these come from Reich, whose recognition that psychological distress was held in chronic muscle tension and could be relieved through breathing, touch and deep massage, is the centre point for all body work. The fairly simple techniques employed by Reich have a very powerful and cathartic effect with the possibilities of enormous emotional release. The fact that Reich was quite mad at the end of his life and died in prison should not blind us to the importance of his work and the importance of his contribution to humanistic and other forms of psychotherapy. Reich went through so many revisions of his work that it is difficult to speak definitively of him, but as he became more and more involved with body work, he left behind him more and more of his early psychoanalytic enthusiasm and focused exclusively on the body.

Alexander Lowen reintroduced the analytic understanding into body work and eventually developed the best known of the body therapies: Bioenergetics.

Gerda Boyesen on the other hand was so involved with the body in therapy that as part of her training as a psychotherapist, she qualified as a physiotherapist.

In *Innovative Therapy in Britain* Rowan and Dryden include three chapters on three separate forms of body work: Bioenergetics, Biodynamic therapy and Biosynthesis. The very similarity of their names seem to suggest to me that their differences are less important than their similarities and that they all share a basic Reichian approach with a greater or lesser degree of analytical understanding and discussion. Interestingly enough, they do not include Rolfing and Postural Integration in their book, although Postural Integration is available in Britain.

CO COUNSELLING

This must be the ultimate in humanistic democratic therapy, because it hardly needs a therapist at all. The system requires that people work together in couples, each taking it in turn to facilitate the other in whatever work he needs to do. Short courses are used to train people in the methods and safety rules of co counselling and then people form their own self help groups.

Co counselling is the only way many people are able to afford any sort of therapy at all and as such must be praised, but like all self help approaches to therapy, it has its limitations and clearly is not a professionally facilitated psychotherapy, but neither does it claim to be. If you have been using this book as an aid to group study, you will have been working within the philosophy of co counselling, which is that the lack of an expert teacher or therapist does not mean you are powerless to learn or to change. Co counselling sees itself particularly as a tool of empowerment for disadvantaged groups. In the present climate of cuts in training budgets, that includes everybody in the helping professions interested in psychotherapy.

THE CREATIVE ARTS THERAPIES

No one has ever doubted the value of the creative arts as therapies. Shakespeare recognised the power of music to "soothe the savage breast" and amateur dramatics have long since been recommended to people with certain sorts of problems as a way out of their problems. Similarly, no one can deny the therapeutic qualities of a good splash with a paint brush or the squeezing and banging of a piece of clay which you then turn into a figure, no matter how amateurish.

The creative arts therapists in all the art forms, both plastic and performance, have developed therapeutic ways of using the arts, but dramatherapy and art therapy in particular have adapted the arts to a specifically psychotherapeutic process. In fact, art psychotherapy is now a recognised form.

The art therapists were the first group to establish themselves and form a professional body with negotiated pay scales in the N.H.S. Their recognised courses and professional requirements have been the models which the other arts therapies have followed.

Art psychotherapy is a process in which the making of images, whether drawn, painted or modelled plays a large part in the therapy. Sometimes the client may come with a feeling or problem which after talking about, becomes the starting point of an image, or even better an image is made while talking about it. At other times the client may start by making the image and discover something about his feeling in the process. The interesting thing about art psychotherapy is that the image gives a physical record of the session which can always be looked at during the session or later. The therapy has plenty of scope for working on feelings both at a cognitive and emotive level as well as possibilities for working with dreams. The art psychotherapist has the possibility to link the making of images to any particular model of psychotherapy, from the psychoanalytic through the Jungian, to Gestalt and the Person Centred Approach.

This is one of the few forms of therapy available in most psychiatric services, although not all art therapists are qualified art psychotherapists.

Dramatherapy has come a long way since I trained. Although there are dramatherapists who do not work psychotherapeutically, those who do, have had a sound training in both drama and therapy and must have proper supervision as a condition of membership of the British Association of Dramatherapists. Dramatherapy has largely been pioneered by Sue Jennings, Gordon Wiseman and Roy Shuttleworth and has drawn its inspiration mainly from Moreno, but also from Sue Jennings' anthropological studies which gave her a wider perspective on drama as a group therapeutic activity. While a dramatherapist is not trained in psychodrama per se, he will probably use a lot of psychodrama techniques. Like everything else, dramatherapy suffers from the Moreno problem. However, dramatherapy tends to have the whole group active a lot of the time and it is a marvellous tool for studying group dynamics. It also offers opportunities for an individual to work on a problem while supported by the group and directed by the dramatherapist. Most dramatherapists tend to work by suggesting exercises for the group. This encourages transference to build up quickly and can often make the groups very lively.

Action and reaction are the bases on which dramatherapy rests and any session will start with warm up exercises to get the group going, some sort of action and finally feed back. A session normally lasts from one and a half to three hours.

Dramatherapists are working more widely in the N.H.S. and their spread should increase with the development of courses and a recognised pay scale. In the main dramatherapy is a group therapy, but some dramatherapists also work with individuals.

Music therapy as I have experienced it, while a very skilled activity, is not a psychotherapy, nor does it claim to be.

Dance Movement therapy in Britain has been a bit late in getting going and has amalgamated under its wing both dance and movement therapists. Some elements of the work are deeply therapeutic, while others are more concerned with movement per se. Dance therapy is an established form of psychotherapy in the U.S.A. and the work of the Moshe Feldenkrais has been very influential in the U.S.A. and in Britain, where people like Helen Payne have been instrumental in setting up a national organisation. (See the address list).

THE INBETWEENIES - OTHER IMPORTANT THERAPIES

There is a group of therapies for which I have some affection and respect although I do not consider them to fall within my definition of psychotherapy. However, I think they are important enough to warrant discussion here.

TRANSACTIONAL ANALYSIS

Transactional Analysis or T.A. as it is normally known, is a form of therapy which has grown out of the writing of Eric Berne. It is often wrongly written off as a superficial and simplified form of psychoanalysis, which it is not.

T.A. is a clearly defined form of therapy which, while not being simplistic, is simple to understand. It is best known for its concept of Games and for its division of behaviour into the forms of parent, adult and child. T.A. is a method in itself, but also an approach to thinking about life problems which can be used in conjunction with other therapeutic approaches.

In researching T.A. for this book, I have become aware how superficial my own knowledge of the subject is. T.A. is to some extent a victim of its own success, because words like strokes and games playing have become buzz words and a part of the therapeutic language and in so doing have had their specific T.A. meanings perverted.

T.A. has been taken up by many people in the caring professions, especially those working in the community like social workers and community nurses, because of its ease of use and efficacy as a problem solving tool. However, whether it can be viewed as a psychotherapy in the sense used in this book is open to question and depends upon how it is used. Where it is used as an aid to solving immediate problems, it is not a psychotherapy, but where it is used as a tool for long term therapy it may well be. There are training programmes in T.A. in Britain and some of these aim to qualify people to give long term psychotherapy using T.A.

COUNSELLING

This is a problematic area for us, because the range of activities undertaken under the heading of counselling is so wide. Some definitions of counselling centre on the fact that the counsellor deals with problems on a here and now basis without effecting a long term relationship with the client and without investigating the client's repressed material.

However, there are also many counsellors who have undertaken further training in psychotherapy and who fit very nicely into our definition of what a psychotherapist is. Clearly therefore it is important to look at the individual counsellor and ask if that person is also a psychotherapist or a person who is in fact practising psychotherapy while calling himself a counsellor.

The British Association of Counselling has compiled a directory of counsellors, in which it makes clear that it is up to the client to make sure that he is getting what he wants and in the listings there is space for counsellors to say whether they have supervision, as well as what sort or counselling or therapy they offer.

The B.A.C. also runs a registration scheme for counsellors and a system of registered supervisors.

COUPLES THERAPY AND FAMILY THERAPY

These tend to be problem solving therapies rather than psychotherapies. A couple or family come with a particular presenting problem which the therapist or therapists (there are often two or more) attempt to solve. In finding a solution, the uncovering of repressed material and the development of transference are either discouraged or seen as irrelevant. These therapies tend to be about how families and couples interact and about helping them to interact more effectively. The therapists are often highly trained and work in a team, often using their understanding of unconscious processes in their clinical formulations as well as ideas about systems theory and paradoxical interventions as they react upon cognitive processes. This form of treatment is becoming more widespread in the N.H.S. and social services.

While these therapies are not psychotherapies in our sense of the word and do not claim to be, they are clearly based on an understanding of psychotherapeutic processes. However, most family therapists view the family as a system and work on the basis that something has gone wrong with the relationships within the family system rather than something having gone wrong with the relationship between an individual's conscious and unconscious awareness. Both the forms of family therapy represented by the ideas of Minuchin and also that represented by the Milan School are very clearly worked out systems of therapy which require a rigorous training and can not therefore be carried out by someone who has "read the manual". Unfortunately there are many people like the doctor represented in the chapter CHARLATANS WELL INTENTIONED AND OTHERWISE who like to call themselves family therapists but aren't.

There is also a movement in family therapy, which draws on psychoanalytic concepts, which is much more like the theory of psychotherapy this book is proposing and that has been pioneered by John Cleese's therapist Robin Skynner. This form of therapy gains respectability by its association with Robin Skynner and uses a process similar to that employed in the group analytic method.

Some humanistic psychologists also work with families and couples. Psychodrama can be employed very effectively either to open up a problem which the family cannot discuss or to help family members work dramatically on specific problems which the family view as their own. Of course the humanistic approach tends towards a situation in which therapist and family or couple work out what the problems are together, rather than the therapist giving the family the benefit of his experience and superior knowledge.

In the main, family therapy is limited to a dozen or less meetings over a six to twelve month period, although there are examples of bizarrely long interactions between family and therapist in the literature. The main centre for therapy and training in England is the Family Institute in London.

SEX THERAPY

Psychoanalysis used to be the treatment of choice for sexual dysfunction, but the methods developed by the behavioural therapists are so much quicker and more effective that sex clinics now use these approaches almost exclusively. Interestingly, the behaviourists have been least successful with problems in women. The women's movement has been quick to recognise that this is caused by the fact that often women's sexual problems are caused by the men they have to relate to in a male dominated world (See page 61). Availability on the N.H.S. is quite widespread.

CHAPTER TEN

PSYCHOTHERAPY AND MENTAL ILLNESS

In a review of the first edition, in *Open Mind*, it was pointed out that I used the term "mental illness" without defining what it was. I therefore attempted to write a definition of this term for the second edition and found it to be quite impossible. I realised that like Thomas Szasz in his *Myth of Mental Illness* I was unable to view mental illness as an illness in the commonly accepted sense of an invasion by a damaging foreign body, e.g. a virus, or damage caused by physical impact or natural decay of the body. The problem is compounded by our realisation that the floridly psychotic person and the very depressed person need help and that this help is generally to be found in Mental Hospitals. I by no means intend what follows here to be taken as an assertion that the so-called "mentally ill" don't need help. What I am questioning is firstly whether they are ill in the generally accepted sense of the word and secondly whether their condition can properly be considered the province of the medical profession.

What follows is intended to be a contribution to a discussion, not an essay on *The Myth of Mental Illness* which Szasz has himself done much better.

EXERCISES

Before reading this section it is as well to be aware of your own prejudices and preconceptions about what mental illness is.

EXERCISE ONE

Just for fun you could try writing a short definition of mental illness just to see how difficult it is.

EXERCISE TWO

Try thinking about the difference between someone who is depressed and someone who is ill with a disease like T.B. or chicken pox. Make a list of the similarities and differences e.g.

PHYSICAL ILLNESS	MENTAL ILLNESS
caused by bacteria	not caused by bacteria
treated with drugs	not treated with drugs
etc.	

EXERCISE THREE

Look at the following dialogue.

This is a conversation that I have had many times. While it is not a verbatim account, it is accurate.

Nurse: I don't see the problem in defining mental illness. The hospital is full of mentally ill people.

Me: Are the staff then mentally ill?

Nurse: No, of course not, the nurses are not mentally ill.

Me: But there is a nurse on my ward who is a patient and is receiving E.C.T. and drugs.

Nurse: Well, he is clearly mentally ill, so he isn't functioning as a nurse. He is a mentally ill patient.

Me: So, are you saying that providing a person is functioning as a nurse as opposed to being stopped from functioning because he is a patient that he is not mentally ill?

Nurse: Yes, providing it is mental things which stop him functioning.

Me: So, if he wasn't functioning because he had a broken leg or because he didn't like nursing, that would not be mental illness.

Nurse: Yes of course. The person with a broken leg is physically ill.

Me: And the person who doesn't like nursing?

Nurse: He has made a choice not to go to work. I may disagree with him, but it is his choice.

Me: And if he stays in bed and won't get out and won't talk to anyone for a week or longer?

Nurse: That sounds to me as though he is depressed.

Me: Is that mental illness?

Nurse: It depends how long it goes on for.

Me: How long is long enough?

Nurse: That is a matter of judgement. I can see how your mind is working. In a minute you will start asking me if a priest on retreat is mentally ill.

Me: Yes, I was and I think that your answer would be that it's appropriate for the priest not to talk to people in that context and not for the nurse. Although that leaves out the question of whose judgement, but I think we will come back to that in different ways.

Nurse: I think that we have to look at whether a person's behaviour is appropriate in the context and then make a judgement, but that is the same with all medicine, physical or psychiatric. It is all based on the skill and judgement of the doctor.

Me: I think that I would agree with you there. One way that we identify the mentally ill is by looking at whether their behaviour is appropriate in the context and using our experience of others, who we judge as healthy or sick, to make a comparison and diagnosis.

Nurse: Yes, and if our judgement is that they are mentally ill, we have to help them.

Me: Even against their will?

Nurse: Sometimes, yes. If they are a danger to themselves and/or others, but the legal restrictions on committing people are pretty tight now and we no longer have situations where people are treated against their will unless they are assessed as being a danger to themselves or others by a doctor and a specially trained social worker. In the main though, people who are mentally ill ask for help themselves.

Me: This seems to me to raise several important issues which we need to try and deal with separately. If we go back to our nurse who is not functioning as a nurse and who is an in-patient on a psychiatric ward, we can say that he is mentally ill because he is not functioning in his job. But I have met many people who I would describe as mentally ill, who are indeed functioning in their jobs and some of whom are even psychiatric nurses or psychiatrists.

Nurse: Well, they might be mentally ill, but not have been classified as such.

Me: Yes, I can see that point, but if they are not in hospital or classified as mentally ill, being in a mental hospital is not in itself a definition of mental illness.

Nurse: No, it would seem not and the problem is that many mentally ill people can be treated out in the community, for example with drugs.

Me: Is the trick then that if you need drugs you are mentally ill?

Nurse: No, the key to the question is more to do with whether you feel that you need help with a problem which affects the way that you behave.

Me: It is behaviour then which defines mental illness?

Nurse: Not only behaviour, but also feelings. Often it is because a person says he wants help in the first place, that we realise he is mentally ill.

Me: Yes, I can see that and I think I can agree with you there. It's like we said before: mental illness is a definition we come to through observation of the patient and discussion with the patient of what he is feeling.

Nurse: Yes, it's just like with a physical illness. That's how we do diagnosis in general medicine.

Me: Actually, I am not so sure that it is just like that.

Nurse: Why?

Me: Well, let's assume that I am telling my doctor of symptoms of shortness of breath, a persistent cough and continued fatigue and that these symptoms started after a foreign holiday. He might suspect that I have T.B., but before attempting to start treatment he would want to do scientific tests to ascertain the physical presence of the Tuberculosis bacillus. Similarly if I complain of symptoms consistent with a fracture, he would want to do an X-ray to confirm the diagnosis.

Nurse: Yes, of course, but so what?

Me: Well, there aren't any such bacilli or physical damage in mental illnesses such as depression.

Nurse: No, there aren't, even though it is often possible to identify changes in brain chemistry associated with mental illnesses.

Me: There you go again, calling them illnesses.

Nurse: Isn't that what we are talking about?

Me: Well, if there are no physical causes like there are for physical diseases, why should we talk of mental illness?

Nurse: Are you saying that there is no such thing as mental illness, so we don't need mental hospitals?

Me: Yes, in a way I think I am saying that mental illness, if it exists, is very unlike other illness and does not need the intervention of medical doctors and all the paraphernalia of the medical profession.

Nurse: So why call it mental illness?

Me: Why indeed? It seems to me to be an anachronism which stems from the unbridled power of the medical profession and our assumption that doctors can cure all our ills.

Nurse: So who should deal with the mentally ill?

Me: That is an interesting point. There is probably some space for doctors, but I see the major place for people with a training in psychotherapy, not psychiatry.

Nurse: So if they are not mentally ill, what are these people?

Me: Well, until we have a better term we will probably continue calling them mentally ill, but if we recognise the contradictions in what we are saying, then we will be making progress.

What follows are questions raised by the dialogue above to enable you to understand and develop your own ideas. After the questions I have given my commentary.

1. Is medical help the most appropriate help?

It may well be, that my human feelings of compassion are aroused by seeing someone who is suffering mentally. I cannot avoid the fact that he needs help, but this won't necessarily convince me that he needs medical or psychiatric help. Having seen what goes on in mental hospitals, I often say that I am going to have tattooed on my chest that in the event of my having a nervous breakdown I am to be taken anywhere but to a psychiatric hospital.

2. Is being a danger to myself, i.e. wanting to kill myself, an illness?

We are far from clear about this too. If I want to kill myself by slashing my wrists or taking a drug overdose, I am far more likely to be committed to a hospital than if I choose to do the same thing by refusing to eat. More importantly, if it is wrong for me to want to kill myself, surely that is a moral, not a medical judgement and I should be committed to the care of someone who is an expert in morals.

3. If mental illness is behaving out of context, or if you like, bizarre behaviour, how can we rely on the patient's wanting our help as a diagnostic tool?

If the patient is "mad", then why should more credence be given to the statement "I need help" than to the statement "I don't need help"?

4. People who perceive themselves as ill often want treatment which is no good for them.

For example, recently there has been a lot of talk about people demanding antibiotics from their doctors when their illnesses can't be cured by antibiotics.

There may be other issues that need to be discussed, but these are the main ones. I suggest that in discussing them you may need further information. In order to give this information we will need a working definition of mental illness. I propose a descriptive rather than a prescriptive definition.

The mentally ill are those people who are receiving in-patient or out-patient treatment in a mental hospital or as an out-patient, or treatment from a G.P. for a condition which a doctor diagnoses as a mental illness and which is caused neither by a brain injury or an external biological or chemical agent.

This is a far from satisfactory definition but will help us in our discussion as well as any definition I can think of. Some points which will help you are laid out below.

THE MEDICAL MODEL

It is useful to consider how it comes about that the medical profession has managed to gain and maintain such a stranglehold on psychotherapy. A few hundred years ago the mentally ill were seen as people who were possessed and dealt with accordingly by a combination of church and state powers as if their illness were an evil visited them from outside.

The rise of the medical profession enabled doctors to spread their net far and wide even as far as mental illness. As an understanding of the causes of illness developed in the late 19th century, medicine started to become respectable and this added to its power. After all, men who could heal the sick as consistently as doctors began to be able to do, became very powerful men and, as befits very powerful men, they had to have a powerful code of conduct, the Hippocratic oath.

These powerful men showed that sickness was not caused by sin and therefore that mental sickness was not caused by sin either. If the mentally ill were victims of random illness, just like the physically ill, surely it was correct that doctors should treat them. After all, having gained power over a section of the community, who in his right mind would relinquish it?

For a long time doctors were little more than quacks in relation to the mentally ill, but as science produced the "miracles" of insulin shock, ECT and mind bending drugs, it was clearly the medical profession which was best suited to continue to treat the mentally ill.

So long as the mentally ill are seen as suitable for treatment by drugs and physical methods, then doctors are going to be seen as the best people to treat them. However, if a non-medical model of mental illness is adopted, there can be no reason for assuming that doctors are a necessary part of psychotherapy.

In the early days of the development of psychotherapy it was thought that those in the medical profession might have advantages as psychotherapists because of their experience of confidentiality and the Hippocratic oath, also that their knowledge of physical illness would help them to distinguish mental from physical illness.

The problem now seems to be that having once taken possession of mental illness and defining it in medical terms, the doctors are unable to refer to a different sort of model in understanding it.

The medical model takes the view that there is a sick patient who is in need of treatment and cure by a competent and knowledgeable medical practitioner. Many people attempt to do psychotherapy using just such a model. However, this is hardly a tenable approach once it is understood that mental illness is not an illness in the usual sense of the word. The model I prefer in doing psychotherapy is one in which the therapist and the person who has come for help work co-operatively to try and understand the nature of the problem, how it has come about and how to resolve it. In this model the patient can be seen more accurately as a client and cure is replaced as an objective by resolution. It now becomes clear that the client is not engaging in therapy to receive a cure from the knowledgeable therapist and that the word cure is therefore totally out of place in therapy. If the job of a doctor is to cure the sick, then it is clear that he has no place in psychotherapy because therapy has no place for cures.

MENTAL ILLNESS AS A PEJORATIVE TERM

To say that someone is mentally ill is often to imply that he is somehow inferior. Some psychotherapists seem to believe that this is true and it is certainly both an explicit and implicit belief of most people in psychiatry. Unfortunately it is also implicit in those psychotherapies such as psychoanalysis which persist in using the term patient. The view that mental illness is something to be ashamed of is certainly still the belief of the person on the Clapham omnibus.

For psychotherapists, who adhere to a medical model of psychotherapy in terms of the sick patient being treated by the healthy therapist, the inferior status of the patient causes no problem. In psychoanalysis his relationship is rarely,

if ever, questioned. I find that one of the most irritating elements of psychoanalysis is that psychoanalysts writing about their practice seem unable to avoid
a superiority and smugness both in relationship to themselves and their method.
I have written about this in my *Therapist's Bibliography, 1988 Update*.

The humanistic psychology movement takes a much more co-operative
view of the process of psychotherapy which eschews the medical model and refuses to use the word patient. Once the medical model has been replaced with
one which values the client as an equal, the notion of mental illness has to fly
out of the window and an explanation of psychological dis-ease has to be introduced which explains symptoms as an understandable reaction to intolerable
circumstances and pressures.

Both inside psychiatry and outside there is an increasing awareness of the
dangers involved in labelling people and a lot of effort is often put into trying
not to label patients. If I am right in thinking that the label mentally ill means
little or nothing, the sooner we stop using it, the better.

THE MENTALLY ILL AS FRIGHTENING

Emotionally disturbed people can be frightening, either because they are
physically violent or because they do not conform to the usual norms of polite
behaviour.

In either case they seem to have lost the ability or the wish to exert the
usual inhibiting controls on their behaviour and this can make them very difficult to control. Where people are offering or threatening physical violence, it
is very difficult to know how to deal with them. Their carers, not surprisingly,
often opt for the safest route which may not be the one which is best for the
client.

The people who are not physically violent may threaten their carer just as
powerfully because they threaten the complacency with which the people paid
to care for them surround themselves. To become mentally ill is in some ways
to finally admit that the pressures are too great and give up the struggle. It may
well be that the people paid to care for them are themselves waging the same
struggle and find their own stability threatened by this giving up. They may also
feel attacked, because the people they are caring for have chosen to stop telling the lie that everything is O.K.

THE MENTALLY ILL PUT US IN TOUCH WITH OUR OWN PAIN

In my experience of working in psychiatry, there is a great conspiracy of silence amongst the staff, who seem to have no way of coping with the fact that they are often suffering from many of the same syndromes of unhappiness as their patients. This can mean that at the very moment when they are "treating" depressed patients, they are suffering clinical depressions themselves or while attributing a women's marital problems to the fact that she denies her husband a normal sex life be doing the very same thing themselves. This strikes me as a case of the blind leading the blind. I wish I could say that these were isolated cases but I was always amazed when working in the N.H.S. just how similar the problems of the patients were to the problems of the staff. The difference was that the patients acknowledged the reality of their situation and sought help or had it forced upon them while the staff denied their situation and hid it from those who might have been able to help. The power structure of the mental hospital is such, that to admit that you have problems of your own is to jeopardise your job.

WOMEN AND MENTAL ILLNESS

I have referred elsewhere to feminist therapy and inherent in the feminist approach to therapy is an assumption that many of the problems which women experience, which are called mental illness, are actually problems caused by the values of the society in which we live. Take, for example, a woman with three children living at the top of a tower block who is actually trapped indoors most of the day. Her husband returns from work in the evening expecting his dinner and then goes out to the pub. It is hardly surprising when this woman presents at a doctor's surgery with depression. It seems to me that the feminist argument makes perfect sense: This woman's problems are not that she is depressed, but that she is a drudge. You may disagree with this viewpoint but it does require thinking about before it is dismissed out of hand and the woman is sent on her way with a packet of "mother's little helpers".

THE MYTH OF MENTAL ILLNESS

Thomas Szasz has written at some length about the myth of mental illness by which he does not intend us to believe that the mentally ill are not suffering, but rather that the mentally ill are not ill in the accepted sense of the word. Clearly a person with depression is not suffering from a physical injury or a bacterial or viral invasion of the body. Szasz therefore demands of us that we look at the way in which we think about mental illness in a totally new way. He points out many of the inconsistencies in the way we think and talk about mental illness.

Psychotherapy and psychotherapeutic methods are not as such medical methods and while they may have become associated in the public mind with doctors, there is no real reason why doctors should come into the picture at all. There used to be an argument that the Hippocratic oath in some way guaranteed the confidentiality and safety of the patient, but as much of this book is taken up with pointing out the mess that doctors make when they try and meddle in psychotherapy, that argument does not hold water.

A SUMMARY AND SUGGESTION

The mentally ill are not ill in a way which is in any way similar to those who are physically ill and it is therefore unfortunate that their treatment has been taken over by the medical profession whose methods are inappropriate. It is my suggestion that mental illness should be viewed as the province of the psychotherapist and doctors and their methods should only be introduced where there is a need for medical intervention.

This would get the mentally ill out of hospitals where they are victims of their illness and into some other form of care where they could participate in their own recovery. I suggest that this would best be established in therapeutic communities staffed by people with an appropriate and specialist training, not by people such as doctors, nurses and social workers who have adapted their skills to working with the mentally ill.

If mental illness were no longer associated with doctors and nurses, the terms "mental illness" and "the mentally ill" might be replaced with something more accurate like the emotionally disturbed. This would allow the punitive element involved in the medical treatment of these people to wither.

CHAPTER ELEVEN

TRAINING TO BE A PSYCHOTHERAPIST

As this book has placed so much emphasis on the importance of training for psychotherapists, some of the content of this chapter has already been covered. However, the subject is so important that I am taking this risk of repeating myself.

Psychotherapy is an art, not a science which must be studied in depth before it can be practised and this study includes theoretical work, personal therapy and supervised practice.

The setting up of the U.K. Standing Committee for Psychotherapy has highlighted the need for training among psychotherapists. At the moment the assumption is that once statutory regulations comes into force, psychotherapists already practising will be accepted as qualified and that after a certain date the only route to qualification will be through a recognised training programme.

For years the only recognised training programmes were those run under the auspices of the main psychoanalytic and analytic organisations. This meant that the only way to practice as a psychoanalyst, for example, was to fulfil the criteria for training and membership set down by the British Psychoanalytic Society. Similarly there was a qualification available from the Institute of Group Analysis and also for Jungian therapists. However, while these qualifications were highly respected in the professions, they had no legal status. They also had the effect of limiting qualifications to psychoanalytically orientated therapists.

In the last few years there has been a development of training programmes which has created a much wider field of choice. All the major schools and types of psychotherapy have their own training programmes and regulatory systems. There are dozens of training bodies, a range of courses, from the introductory to the fully fledged professional qualification. There is no longer any excuse for practising psychotherapy without training on the grounds that training is not available.

THE U.K. STANDING CONFERENCE FOR PSYCHOTHERAPY

In the 1980s, prompted by the scare over Scientology, which had precipitated very narrow and unconsidered legislation in Australia, and the subsequent Sieghart report in this country, many psychotherapists feared Government interference and the imposition of controls on psychotherapists. The Sieghart report was heavily slanted in the direction of psychoanalysis and other psychotherapists feared that their views would not be considered.

Out of this fear emerged the Rugby Conference, which was organised by the British Association for Counselling, as a neutral body acceptable to all those attending. This became an annual meeting.

The aim was to try and set standards for training and qualifications in psychotherapy. At the end of the decade, the Rugby Conference was properly constituted as an organisation, and changed its name to the U.K. Standing Conference for Psychotherapy. At this point the B.A.C. stepped out of the organisational role it had been taking, and became just an interested observer. So the UKSCP is now an autonomous body, and contains within it virtually all the training organisations in this country which try to produce fully qualified psychotherapists. It also includes representatives of the so- called core professions, in the shape of the Royal College of Psychiatry, the British Psychological Society and the British Association of Social Workers. This is really quite remarkable, and such a thing exists in no other country in the world. At present the Government says it has no plans to regulate psychotherapists, but the UKSCP would be the natural organisation for the Government to consult should that day come.

1992 AND EUROPE

Obviously many people are worried about 1992, when professional qualifications are to be mutually recognised across Europe. There are widely different standards throughout Europe, some very stringent and exclusive and others more liberal.

The UKSCP is working on a number of levels to make sure that the variety of psychotherapies is recognised.

The UKSCP also wants to make it clear that psychotherapy is not part of medicine or of psychology or of social work: hence it is unacceptable to make such qualifications necessary for psychotherapy. In many parts of Europe non-medical psychotherapists are called "lay therapists" and are not allowed to call themselves psychotherapists or to get jobs as psychotherapists. It has been suggested that they should instead be called "independently qualified psychotherapists" and admitted to all the facilities of medical psychotherapists, provided that appropriate ethical and other control can be demonstrated.

The advice to anyone working or intending to work as a psychotherapist is therefore to link up with an organisation, such as the UKSCP, which is paying attention to these problems and hopefully solving them.

A list of useful training addresses is given at the end of this chapter.

BASIC TRAINING REQUIREMENTS

Theory

The practice of psychotherapy seems to go hand in glove with a desire to write about it. The more innovative the therapist thinks his work is, the stronger seems to be the need to write about it. This means that there is no shortage of books about therapy written by practitioners who are anxious to share their own ideas with a wider public. All forms of therapy have a range of literature which explain the underlying psychological theory applicable to the method and how the method is to be applied.

In view of the wide availability of such literature it might seem strange that I do not place emphasis on reading this literature. In fact, some therapists like their clients to avoid reading about the theory of the method while they are in therapy. The reason for this is that psychotherapy is an activity which can best be understood by experiencing it at first hand and knowing too much of the theory can detract from the first hand experience.

However, there would be a certain intellectual dishonesty in ignoring the theoretical underpinning of psychotherapy and therefore obviously there has to be a place in training for reading and discussion of theoretical matters. Also a firm understanding of the psychological model upon which the therapy is based is essential for the therapist's own confidence in carrying out the therapy.

Therapy

The only way to learn about psychotherapy is through experiencing it. Therefore, before offering himself as a psychotherapist, the individual must first have had extensive therapy himself. This serves two functions. The first is that the therapy serves as a giant spring cleaning for the therapist's own psyche, which enables him to clear out and understand his own unconscious processes. Without this clear-out the therapist will not have a deep enough understanding of himself to be able to maintain the right balance of objectivity and subjectivity towards the client. If this balance is not maintained, the therapist is in danger of allowing his own psyche to interact with the client in a way which might not only be unhelpful, but also dangerous.

This second function of the psychotherapist's own therapy is to prepare and strengthen him for the powerful material and emotions which therapy evokes in both the client and the therapist.

Objectivity is very important in psychotherapy and the function of the training therapy is to allow the therapist to face up to the painful and conflicting emotions in his own psyche, which might prevent him being objective about the client he is working with. Much of our subjectivity comes from unconscious forces of which we are unaware and a lengthy experience of subjectivity in the training therapy helps us to be more objective later. This is because the training therapy allows us to get to the root causes of our own subjectivity and to accept our own feelings and emotions. From this position of self acceptance it is far easier to listen to another person objectively. The fact that we have another person there to listen to us and feed back to us, sharpens that objectivity and it is now clear to us that the training therapy requires both a therapist and a therapee. Freud's own analysis through which he discovered and formed his own ideas was a self analysis and therefore many of his ideas are highly subjective. Many of the faults and failings inherent in the psychoanalytic model can be seen to have their source in the subjectivity of Freud's own self analysis. In the early stages of psychoanalysis he thought that operation of the techniques of psychoanalysis was sufficient, but as he built up a body of followers it became apparent that they needed personal therapy more than they needed instruction in technique.

Reich, although he later was expelled from the psychoanalytic movement, was instrumental in demonstrating the need for the training analysis and starting the first training programmes. This is described very clearly in Sharaf's compelling biography of Reich.

Most training courses in psychotherapy have a minimum requirement for therapy and some of the best courses offer group therapy as a training therapy while insisting or advising students that they should also have regular personal therapy with a recognised therapist. I want to highlight here the fact that psychotherapy, even in the form of psychoanalysis, does not recognise the possibility of an individual so perfect in himself that he can have nothing to learn from his own therapy. This notion therefore that you have to be mad to require or to benefit from therapy is not one which is consistent with psychotherapeutic thinking. The fact that some people, who may be classified as sick can be helped by therapy does not mean that you have to be sick to require therapy or that benefiting from it means that you are sick.

Supervision

Once the therapist has concluded a reasonable period of personal therapy and has a good grasp of the theory, it is necessary for him to start in supervised practice. You may think that someone who is viewed as qualified should know what he is doing, but there is an enormous difference in therapy between receiving therapy and reading about it to actually giving it. Offering oneself as a therapist is at first a very stressful activity and the support and encouragement of a good supervisor is indispensable and invaluable. The unconscious is very foxy and the more disturbed the client, the more he will try the therapist's competence and patience. It is the job of the supervisor who is outside the relationship between the client and therapist to distinguish objective from subjective reality and to strengthen the therapist.

No relationship in which feelings are evoked and exchanged can run smoothly and it is the difficult job of the therapist both to share in the relationship with the client and to remain outside it. However experienced the therapist may be, there will always be a client who challenges his objectivity. Just as my judo instructor used to tell me: There will always be an opponent who is stronger than you, so technique is more important than strength; there will always be a client who has the power to overcome you as a therapist and send you scuttling for the aid of a supervisor. In his book *The Fifty Minute Hour* Robert Lindner gives an example of a case where he himself takes on the psychotic fantasy of his patient and while I am no advocate of psychoanalysis I recommend this book to anyone interested in knowing more about what it feels like to be a psychotherapist.

This is the last chapter in the book and it feels quite fitting that in saying goodbye I should be offering a list of addresses from which training can be obtained. I hope that you have found the book enjoyable and helpful and that it has inspired you to go out and get trained as a psychotherapist who knows what psychotherapy is.

ADDRESS LIST

Association of Humanistic Psychology Practitioners,
14 Mornington Grove, London E3 4NS.

British Association for Counselling,
37A Sheep Street, Rugby, Warwickshire, CV21 3BX.

British Association for Dramatherapists,
The Old Mill, Tolpuddle, Dorchester, Dorset DT2 7EX.

British Psychodrama Association,
8 Rahere Road, Cowley, Oxford.

British Association for Psychotherapists,
121 Hendon Lane, London N3.

C G Jung Clinic, Society of Analytical Psychology,
1 Daleham Gardens, London NW3 5BY.

Gale Centre for Creative Therapy,
Whitakers Way, Loughton, Essex IG10 1SQ.

Goldsmiths College, (University of London),
Lewisham Way, London SE14.

Hertfordshire College of Art and Design,
7 Hatfield Road, St Albans, Herts.

Holwell Centre for Psychodrama and Sociodrama,
East Down, Barnstaple, North Devon EX31 4NZ.

Institute of Family Therapy,
43 New Cavendish Street, London W1.

Institute of Group Analysis,
1 Daleham Gardens, London, NW3 5BY.

Institute of Psychotherapy and Social Studies,
5 Lake House, South Hill Park, London, NW3 2SH.

Lincoln Centre and Institute for Psychotherapy,
Lincoln Tower, 77 Westminster Bridge Road, London SE1 7HS.

London Association for Primal Psychotherapists,
18a Laurier Road, London NW5 1SH.

London Centre for Psychotherapy,
19 Fitzjohn Avenue, London, NW3 5JY.

London Institute for the Study of Human Sexuality,
Flat C, Langham Mansions, Earls Court Sq., London SW5 9UH.

metanoia Psychotherapy Training Institute,
13 North Common Road, London W5 3QB.

Society of Analytical Psychology,
1 Daleham Gardens, London NW3 5BY.

Tavistock Clinic,
120 Belsize Lane, London, NW3 5BA.

The Gestalt Centre,
64 Warwick Road, St Albans, Herts, AL1 4DL.D

The Institute of Psychoanalysis,
63 New Cavendish Street, London W1M 7RD.

Westminster Pastoral Foundation,
23 Kensington Square, London W8 5HN.

Women's Therapy Centre,
6 Manor Gardens, London N7.

BIBLIOGRAPHY

Adler, Alfred (1924) *Practice and Theory of Individual Psychology*, Littlefield, Adams, Totowa, New Jersey.

Albery, Nicholas (1983) *How to Save the Body*, Revelaction Press.

d'Ardenne P and Mahtani, A (1989) *Transcultural Counselling in Action*, Sage Publications.

Aveline, M and Dryden, W (eds) (1988) *Group Therapy in Britain*, Open University Press.

Axline, V (1971) *Dibs in Search of Self*, Penguin.

Balint, Michael (1968) *The Basic Fault*, Tavistock Publications, London (reprinted 1979 with a preface by Enid Balint)

Bateson, G (1985) *Steps to an Ecology of Mind*, Ballantine Books, New York.

Berne, Eric (1964) *Games People Play, The Psychology of Human Relationships*, Penguin.

Berne, Eric (1961) *Transactional Analysis in Psychotherapy*, Grove Press, New York.

Bettelheim, Bruno (1974) *A Home for the Heart*, Thames and Hudson.

Bettelheim, Bruno (1983) *Freud and Man's Soul*, Chatto & Windus.

Bion, W R (1961) *Experiences in Groups*, Tavistock.

Blatner, A and Blatner, A (1988) *Foundations of Psychodrama, History, Theory and Practice*, Springer, N.Y. (3rd edition)

Blatner, Howard A (1973) *Acting In*, Springer, N.Y.

Boadella, David (1985) *Wilhelm Reich, The Evolution of His Work*, RKP.

Brown, J A C (1974) *Freud and the Post-Freudians*, Penguin.

Bugenthal, J F T (1967) *The Challenges of Humanistic Psychology*, McGraw Hill.

Campbell, D and Draper, R (1983) *Working with the Milan Method, Twenty Questions*, Institute of Family Therapy, London.

Campbell, D, Draper, R and Huffington, C (1988) *Teaching Systemic Thinking*, Institute of Family Therapy, London.

Casement, Patrick (1985) *On Learning from the Patient*, Tavistock.

Chaplin, Jocelyn (1988) *Feminist Counselling in Action*, Sage.

Chesler, Phyllis (1970) *Women and Madness*, Avon.

Clare, Anthony and Thompson, Sally (1981) *Let's Talk About Me, A Critical Examination of the New Psychotherapies*, BBC.

Clarkson, P (1989) *Gestalt Counselling in Action*, Sage Publications.

Cole, M and Dryden W (eds) (1988) *Sex Therapy in Britain*, Open University Press.

Culley, S (1991) *Integrative Counselling Skills in Action*, Sage Publications.

Dalley, Tessa (Ed) (1987) *Images of Art Therapy New Development in Theory and Practice*, Tavistock.

Dalley, Tessa (Ed) (1986) *Art as Therapy, An Introduction to the use of art as a therapeutic technique*, Tavistock.

Drury, N (1989) *The Elements of Human Potential*, Element Books.

Dryden, W (Ed) (1987) *Therapist's Dilemmas*, Open University Press.

Dryden, W (Ed) (1984) *Key Cases in Psychotherapy*, Croom Helm.

Dryden, W (ed) (1990) *Individual Therapy: A Handbook*, Open University Press.

Dryden W (1985) *Marital Therapy in Britain: Vol 1 Context and Therapeutic Approaches,* Open University Press.

Dryden W (1985) *Marital Therapy in Britain: Vol 2 Special Areas,* Open University Press.

Dryden, W and Spurling, L (eds) (1989) *On Becoming a Psychotherapist*, Routledge.

Dryden, W (ed) (1989) *Key Issues for Counselling in Action*, Sage Publications.

Dryden, W (1989) *Rational-Emotive Counselling in Action*, Sage Publications.

Dryden, W and Gordon J (1989) *What is Rational-Emotive Therapy, A personal and practical guide,* Gale Centre Publications.

Eichenbaum, L and Orbach, S (1985) *Understanding Women*, Penguin.

Eichenbaum, L and Orbach, S (1983) *What do Women Want?*, Fontana.

Ernst, Sheila and Goodison, Lucy (1981) *In Our Own Hands, A Book of Self Help Therapy*, Women's Press.

Evans, R I (Ed) (1975) *Carl Rogers, the Man and His Ideas*, E P Dutton, N Y.

Evison, Rose and Horobin, Richard (1983) *How to Change Yourself and Your World*, Co counselling Phoenix.

Fagan, J and Shephard, I (1970) *Gestalt Therapy Now*, Science and Behaviour.

Fairbairn, W Ronald D (1952) *Psychoanalytical studies of the personality*, Tavistock Publications, London.

Fairbairn, W Ronald D (1954) *An object-relations theory of the personality*, Basic Books, New York.

Foulkes, S H and Anthony, E (1957) *Group Psychotherapy: The Psychoanalytic Approach*, Penguin.

Fox, Jonathan (Ed) (1987) *The Essential Moreno*, Springer, N.Y.

Fransella, F and Dalton, P (1990) *Personal Construct Counselling in Action*, Sage Publications.

Freed, A and M (1985) *The New TA for Kids, Powerful Techniques for Developing Self Esteem*, Jalmar Press, Sacramento.

Freud, S (1962) *Case Histories 1: Dora and Little Hans*, Penguin.

Freud, S (1971) *Introductory Lectures on Psychoanalysis*, Penguin.

Freud, S (1969) *New Introductory Lectures on Psychoanalysis*, Penguin.

Freud, S (1955) *The Interpretation of Dreams*, Penguin.

Freud, S with Breuer, J (1956) *Studies on Hysteria*, Penguin.

Gale, D (1987) *A Therapist's Bibliography and Updates*, Gale Centre Pubs.

Gale, D and Shuttleworth, R (1985) *Family Therapy, The Milan Systemic Approach, Tape and Booklet*, Gale Centre Pubs.

Gale, D (1986) *Bereavement and Loss, Tape and Booklet*, Gale Centre Pubs.

Gale, D (1990) *What is Psychodrama, a personal and practical guide*, Gale Centre Pubs.

Gobal, F (1970) *The Third Force*, Grossman, New York.

Goffman, E (1970) *Asylums*, Penguin.

Greenberg, I (Ed) (1974) *Psychodrama: Theory and Therapy*, Condor.

Grof, Stan (1985) *Beyond the Brain: Birth, death and transcendence in psychotherapy*, State University of New York Press.

Guggenbuhl-Craig, A (1986) *Power in the Helping Professions*, Spring.

Guntrip, Harry (1971) *Psychoanalytic theory, therapy and the self*, Basic Books, New York (reprinted 1977 by Maresfield Reprints, London)

Haley, J (1985) *Problem Solving Therapy*, Harper & Row.

Hall, C S and Nordby, V J (1986) *A Primer of Jungian Psychology*, Croom Helm.

Hawkins, P and Shohet R (1989) *Supervision in the Helping Professions: An Individual, Group and Organizational Approach*, Open University Press.

Hillman, James (1977) *Re-Visioning Psychology*, Harper Colophon.

Hillman, James (1978) *Loose Ends, Primary Papers in Archetypal Psychology*, Spring Publications.

Hillman, James (1979) *The Dream and the Underworld*, Harper & Row.

Hinshelwood, Robert D (1989) *A Dictionary of Kleinian Thought*, Free Association Books, London.

Holmes, P and Karp, M (1991) *Psychodrama: Inspiration and Technique*, Routledge.

Horney, Karen (1942) *Self Analysis*, RKP.

Houston, Gaie (1987) *The Red Book of Groups*, Rochester Foundation.

Houston, Gaie (1982) *The Red Book of Gestalt*, Rochester Foundation.

Houston, Gaie (1990) *Supervision and Counselling*, Rochester Foundation.

Jacobi, M (1984) *The Analytic Encounter, Transference and Human Relationship*, Inner City Books.

Jacobs, Michael (1988) *Psychodynamic Counselling in Action*, Sage.

Janov, A (1970) *The Primal Scream*, Putnam, New York.

Janov, A (1971) *The Anatomy of Mental Illness*, Putnam, New York.

Janov, A (1991) *The New Primal Scream*, Abacus.

Jennings, Sue (1987) *Dramatherapy: Theory and Practice for Teachers and Clinicians*, Croom Helm.

Jennings, Sue (1986) *Creative Drama in Groupwork*, Winslow Press.

Jennings, Sue (1978) *Remedial Drama, A Handbook for Teachers and Therapists*, Pitman.

Jennings, Sue (Ed) (1988) *Creative Therapy*, Kemble Press (2nd edition).

Johnson, D W and Johnson, F A (1982) *Joining Together, Group Theory and Group Skills*, Prentice Hall Inc, New Jersey. (2nd edition)

Jung, C G (1960) *Modern Man in Search of a Soul*, RKP.

Jung, C G (1954) *The Practice of Psychotherapy, Essays on the Psychology of Transference and other subjects*, Pantheon Books.

Jung, C G (1957) *Memories, Dreams, Reflections*, Flamingo.

Jung, C G (1965) *The Psychology of Transference*, RKP.

Jung, C G (1964) *Man and his Symbols*, Picador.

Kempler, Walter (1973) *Principles of Gestalt Family Therapy*, Gardner.

Kernberg, Otto (1976) *Object relations theory and clinical psychoanalysis*, Jason Aronson, New York.

Kesey, Ken (1962) *One Flew over the Cuckoo's Nest*, New American Library.

Klein, Melanie (1974) *Collected Works*, Hogarth Press.

Kline, P (1972) *Fact and Fantasy in Freudian Theory*, Methuen.

Kirschenbaum, H and Land Henderson, V (1990) *Carl Rogers Dialogues*, Constable.

Kirschenbaum, H and Land Henderson, V (1990) *Carl Rogers Reader*, Constable.

Kohon, Grigorio (1986) *The British school of psychoanalysis: The independent tradition*, Free Association Books, London.

Kovel, Joel (1978) *A Complete Guide to Therapy*, Penguin.

Laing, R D (1983) *The Voice of Experience*, Penguin.

Laing, R D (1967) *The Politics of Experience and The Bird of Paradise*, Penguin.

Laing, R D (1969) *Self and Others*, Penguin.

Laing, R D (1967) *The Divided Self*, Penguin.

Laing, R D and Esterson, A (1970) *Sanity, Madness and the Family*, Penguin.

Lake, F (1986) *Clinical Theology*, Darton, Longman and Todd (2nd edition).

Lakin Phillips, E (1977) *Counselling and Psychotherapy: A Behavioural Approach*, Wiley.

Leveton, Eva (1977) *Psychodrama for the Timid Clinician*, Springer Publishing Co.

Lieberman, Marian (1986) *Art Therapy for Groups, A Handbook of Themes, Games and Exercises*, Croom Helm.

Lindner, Robert (1987) *The Fifty Minute Hour*, Free Association Books.

LoPiccolo, J and LoPiccolo, L (1978) *Handbook of Sex Therapy*, Plenum Press, New York.

Lowen, A (1975) *Bioenergetics*, Penguin.

Lowen, A & L (1977) *The Way to Vibrant Health: A Manual of Bioenergetic Exercises*, Harper Colophon.

Mahrer, Alvin (1978) *Experiencing: A humanistic theory of psychology and psychiatry*, Brunner/Mazel.

Maslow, A (1971) *The Farther Reaches of Human Nature*, Penguin.

Maslow, A H (1962) *Toward a Psychology of Being*, Van Nostrand Reinhold, New York.

Masson, J W Moussaieff (1984) *The Assault on Truth, Freud's suppression of the Seduction Theory*, Farrar, Strauss and Giroux.

Masson, J W Moussaieff (1991) *Final Analysis, The Making and Unmaking of a Psychoanalyst*, HarperCollins.

McGuire, William (Ed) (1974) *The Freud/Jung Letters*, Hogarth Press and Routledge & Kegan Paul.

Mearns, D and Thorne, B (1988) *Person-Centred Counselling in Action*, Sage.

Merry, Tony (1988) *A Guide to the Person-Centred Approach*, AHPB.

Miller, A (1988) *The Drama of Being a Child*, Virago.

Miller, Alice (1985) *Thou Shalt Not Be Aware, Society's Betrayal of the Child*, Pluto Press.

Miller, Alice (1987) *For Your Own Good, The Roots of Violence in Child Rearing*, Virago.

Miller, Alice (1990) *Banished Knowledge, Facing Childhood Injuries*, Virago.

Miller, Jean Baker (1978) *Towards a New Psychology of Women*, Penguin.

Mindell, A (1985) *Working with the Dreaming Body*, RKP.

Minuchin, S (1974) *Families and Family Therapy*, Tavistock.

Mitchell, Juliet (1987) *Psychoanalysis and Feminism*, Penguin.

Mitchell, Juliet (1988) *Selected Melanie Klein*, Penguin.

Moore, T (ed) (1990) *The Essential James Hillman: A Blue Fire*, Routledge.

Moreno, J L (1975) *The Theatre of Spontaneity*, Beacon House, New York.

Moreno, J L (1969) *Psychodrama, Vol 1 - 3*, Beacon House, New York.

Munro, E, Manthei, R J and Small S J (1980) *Counselling, a skills approach*, Methuen.

Parry, R (1985) *Basic Psychotherapy*, Churchill Livingstone.

Payne, H (1990) *Creative Movement and Dance in Groupwork*, Winslow Press.

Perls, F S, Hefferline, R and Goodman, P (1970) *Gestalt Therapy, Excitement and Growth in the Human Personality*, Penguin.

Perls, F (1969) *Gestalt Therapy Verbatim*, Real People Press, Moab, Utah.

Porter, Roy (1987) *Mind-Forg'd Manacles - A History of Madness in England*, Athlone Press.

Porter, Roy (1987) *A Social History of Madness: Stories of the Insane*, Weidenfield and Nicholson.

Reich, W (1950) *Character Analysis*, Vision.

Reich, W (1942) *The Function of the Orgasm*, World Publishing.

Reich, W and Neill, A S (19) *Record of a Friendship. The Correspondence between W Reich and A S Neill*, Gollancz.

Ridgway, Roy (1987) *The Unborn Child: How to recognize and overcome parental trauma*, Wildwood House.

Ridgway, R (1990) *Caring for Your Unborn Child*, Thorsons.

Rioch, Margaret (1961) *Dialogues for Therapists*, Jossey-Bass, San Francisco.

Rogers, C (1970) *Encounter Groups*, Penguin.

Rogers, C (1967) *On Becoming a Person, A Therapist's View of Psychotherapy*, Constable.

Rogers, C (1965) *Client Centred Therapy*, Constable.

Rowan, J (1988) *Ordinary Ecstasy*, RKP.

Rowan, J (1983) *The Reality Game: A guide to humanistic counselling and therapy*, RKP.

Rowan, J (1987) *A Guide to Humanistic Psychology*, AHPB.

Rowan J and Dryden, W (eds) (1988) *Innovative Therapy in Britain*, Open University Press.

Rowe, Dorothy (1988) *Depression, The Way Out of Your Prison*, RKP.

Rowe, Dorothy (1991) *The Depression Handbook*, HarperCollins.

Satir, V (1970) *Conjoint Family Therapy, A Guide to Theory and Technique*, Souvenir Press.

Satir, V (1972) *Peoplemaking*, Science and Behaviour.

Schaffer, J B P and Galinski, M D (1974) *Models of Group Therapy and Sensitivity Training*, Prentice-Hall.

Schutz, W (1967) *Joy: Expanding Human Awareness*, Souvenir Press.

Schutz, W (1971) *Here Comes Everybody*, Harper & Row, New York.

Schutz, W (1973) *Elements of Encounter*, Joy Press.

Segal, Hanna (1975) *Introduction to the Work of Melanie Klein*, Hogarth Press.

Selvini-Palazzoli et al (1978) *Paradox and Counter Paradox*, Jason Aronson.

Sharaf, M (1982) *Fury on Earth, A Biography of Wilhelm Reich*, Hutchinson.

Shohet, Robin (1985) *Dream Sharing*, Turnstone Press.

Showalter, Elaine (1985) *The Female Malady. Women, Madness and English Culture*, Virago.

Skynner, Robin A C (1988) *One Flesh, Separate Persons. Principles of Family and Marital Psychotherapy*, Constable.

Skynner, Robin and Cleese, John (1987) *Families and How to Survive Them*, Methuen.

Southgate, J and Randall, R (1978) *The Barefoot Psychoanalyst, an illustrated manual of self help*, Gale Centre Publications (3rd edition).

Southgate, J and Whiting, L (1987) *Self Analysis, Vol 1, No 1, The Journal of the Institute for Self Analysis*, Institute of Self Analysis.

Stevens, Richard (1987) *Freud and Psychoanalysis*, Croom Helm.

Stewart, I (1989) *Transactional Analysis Counselling in Action*, Sage Publications

Stewart, I and Joines, V (1989) *TA Today: A New Introduction to Tranactional Analysis*, Lifespace Publishing.

Storr, Anthony (1973) *Jung*, Fontana.

Street, E and Dryden W (1988) *Family Therapy in Britain*, Open University Press.

Szasz, Thomas S (1965) *The Myth of Psychotherapy*, Garden City, New York, Doubleday.

Szasz, Thomas S (1961) *The Myth of Mental Illness*, Secker & Warburg.

Thomas, D M (1980) *The White Hotel*, Penguin.

Trower, P and Dryden, W (1988) *Cognitive-Behavioural Counselling in Action*, Sage Publications.

Vaughan, Frances (1986) *The Inward Arc, Healing and Wholeness in Psychotherapy and Spirituality*, Shambhala.

Verny, Tom with Kelly, John (1987) *The Secret Life of the Unborn Child*, Sphere.

Walrond-Skinner, Sue (1982) *Developments in Family Therapy*, RKP.

Walrond-Skinner, Sue (1986) *A Dictionary of Psychotherapy*, RKP.

Watts, Alan (1951) *Psychotherapy East and West*, Pantheon, New York.

Watts, Alan (1957) *The Way of Zen*, Pantheon Books.

Watts, Alan (1970) *The Book on the Taboo Against Knowing Who You Are*, Abacus.

Wilber, K, Engler and Brown (1986) *Transformations of Consciousness*, New Science Library, Boston.

Wilber, K (1981) *No Boundary, Eastern and Western Approaches to Personal Growth*, RKP.

Williams, Antony (1989) *The Passionate Technique, Strategic Psychodrama with Individuals, Families and Groups*, Routledge.

Winnicott, Donald W (1971) *Playing and Reality*, Tavistock Publications, London (reprinted 1980 by Penguin Books)

Winnicott, D W (1983) *The Piggle, An Account of the Psychoanalytical treatment of a little girl*, Penguin.

Yablonsky, L (1975) *Psychodrama, Resolving Emotional Problems Through Role Playing*, Basic Books, New York.

Yalom, I D (1985) *The Theory and Practice of Group Psychotherapy*, Basic Books Inc, New York.

OTHER BOOKS IN THIS SERIES:

WHAT IS PSYCHODRAMA, A personal and practical guide, *Derek Gale, £5.95.*

ISBN 1 870258 07 X, 136 pages.

The first British introduction to Psychodrama, a much used action therapy in groupwork, invented 60 years ago by J.L. Moreno. Derek Gale is well known for his Psychodrama workshops; he writes in a very personal style which makes the techniques easy to understand.

WHAT IS RATIONAL-EMOTIVE THERAPY, A personal and practical guide, *Windy Dryden and Jack Gordon, £5.95.*

ISBN 1 870258 08 8, 96 pages.

Windy Dryden explains in a way that is accessible to both therapists and lay-people what exactly is meant by Rational- Emotive Therapy, its principles, methodology and techniques. Can be used for a peer-study group or individual use. Dr Windy Dryden is THE British expert on the subject. According to the Counselling Journal of the British Association for Counselling, this is the best introductory text on RET!

IN PREPARATION:

WHAT IS TRANSACTIONAL-ANALYSIS, A personal and practical guide, *Eric Whitton, £5.95.*

ISBN 1 870258 24 X, 100 pages. Publication Date: January 1992.

Eric Whitton has been teaching and running workshops on Transactional Analysis for many years. He is one of the core trainers at the Open Centre in London, a well known organisation for long and short term therapy courses. Like the other books in the series, this is both personal and practical.

For full details write to:

GALE CENTRE PUBLICATIONS WHITAKERS WAY LOUGHTON, ESSEX IG10 1SQ. Tel: (081) 508 9344 FAX: (081) 508 1240